HOUGHTON MIFF

English

Authors
Robert Rueda
Tina Saldivar
Lynne Shapiro
Shane Templeton
C. Ann Terry
Catherine Valentino
Shelby A. Wolf

Consultants
Jeanneine P. Jones
Monette Coleman McIver
Rojulene Norris

HOUGHTON MIFFLIN   BOSTON

Acknowledgments

For each of the selections listed below, grateful acknowledgment is made for permission to excerpt and/or reprint original or copyrighted material as follows:

Published Models

"A New House" from *Grasshopper on the Road* by Arnold Lobel. Copyright ©1978 by Arnold Lobel. Used by permission of HarperCollins Publishers.

"A Very Special Day" adapted from *Pablo's Tree* by Pat Mora, illustrated by Cecily Lang. Text copyright ©1994 by Pat Mora. Illustrations copyright ©1994 by Cecily Lang. Reprinted with the permission of Simon & Schuster Books for Young Readers, an imprint of Simon & Schuster Children's Publishing Division.

"Pop-Up Flower Card" adapted from *Your Big Backyard Magazine*, March 1999 issue, a publication of the National Wildlife Federation. Copyright ©1999 by National Wildlife Federation. Adapted by permission of National Wildlife Federation.

"A Winter Day" from *Winter* by Ron Hirschi, photographs by Thomas D. Mangelsen. Text copyright ©1990 by Ron Hirschi. Photographs copyright ©1990 by Thomas D. Mangelsen. Used by permission of Cobblehill Books, an affiliate of Dutton Children's Books, a division of Penguin Putnam Inc.

Poetry

"Beetle" by Sylvia Gerdtz from *Big Dipper Rides Again* edited by June Epstein, June Factor, Gwendola McKay & Dorothy Richards (O.U.P. Australia). Reprinted by permission of June Factor on behalf of the editors.

"The Crocus" by Walter Crane.

"First Snow" from *A Pocketful of Poems* by Marie Louise Allen. Text copyright 1957 by Marie Allen Howarth. Used by permission of HarperCollins Publishers.

"Smile" from *Bing Bang Boing* by Douglas Florian. Copyright ©1994 by Douglas Florian. Reprinted with permission of Harcourt, Inc.

"Toaster Time" from *There Is No Rhyme for Silver* by Eve Merriam. Copyright ©1962, 1990 by Eve Merriam. Used by permission of Marian Reiner for the author.

"Tommy" from *Bronzeville Boys and Girls* by Gwendolyn Brooks. Copyright ©1956 by Gwendolyn Brooks Blakely. Used by permission of HarperCollins Publishers.

Acknowledgments are continued on page 325.

ISBN-13: 978-0-618-61117-1
ISBN-10: 0-618-61117-7

19 20 0877 21 20 19 18 17 16 15 14

4500492489

HOUGHTON MIFFLIN
English

Just turn the page.
Then follow the colors.

Grammar units are blue.

Look for these ways to make to your writing better.

Proofreading

Think and Write

Revising Strategies

Writing units are green.

Use these grammar links for help as you write.

GRAMMAR CHECK

Proofreading Checklist

Look for these parts, too!

Special Focus

COMMUNICATION LINK

Tools and Tips are in the red part.

Find these pages at the back of your book.

- Research and Study Strategies
- Using Technology
- Letter Models
- Word Finder
- My Picture Dictionary
- Opposites
- Handwriting Models

Visit Kids' Place for Houghton Mifflin English at www.eduplace.com/kids/hme for activities like these.

- Bright Ideas for Writing
- Grammar Blast
- Evaluation Station
- Net's Best for Research
- Authors and Illustrators
- Graphic Organizers
- Writers' Showcase

2A

TABLE OF CONTENTS

Unit 7 Adjectives 172

Unit 8 Writing a Description 190

Unit 9 — More Capitalization and Punctuation 216

Unit 10 — Writing Instructions 246

Special Focus 274

Tools and Tips 292

Listening, Speaking, Viewing, and Writing

We listen, speak, view, and write every day. What might these people be listening to, saying, viewing, or writing?

Name

Listening

Why We Listen

We listen for many reasons.

 Why are these people listening?

 Circle a picture that shows one way you listen.

 Talk about why you listen.

How We Listen

 Talk about the tips for listening.

Tips for Listening

★ Listen carefully to the words.

★ Think about what you hear.

★ Look at the speaker's face and hands.

★ Raise your hand and ask questions.

Apply It

Draw pictures of yourself following the listening tips.

Name _____

Speaking

Why We Speak

We speak for many reasons.

 Why are these people speaking?

 ▶ Circle a picture that shows one way you speak.

 Talk about why you speak.

How We Speak

 Talk about the tips for speaking.

Tips for Speaking

★ Look at your listeners.

★ Speak clearly and loudly enough.

★ Use your face and hands to help show what you mean.

Apply It

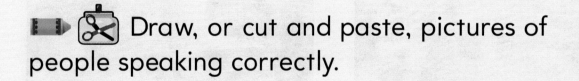 Draw, or cut and paste, pictures of people speaking correctly.

Name _____

Viewing

Why We View

Viewing is looking and thinking about what we see. We view for many reasons.

 Why are these people viewing?

✏️ Circle the pictures that show ways you view.

🔲 Talk about why you view.

How We View

 Talk about the tips for viewing.

Tips for Viewing

★ Look at the whole picture or object. Then look at each part.

★ Ask yourself questions about what you see.

★ Think about the message or main idea.

Apply It

Color the picture that shows all of the children using the tips for viewing.

Talk about the picture you did <u>not</u> color. Which tip are some viewers not following?

Name _____

Writing

Why We Write

We write for many reasons.

 Why are these children writing?

 Circle the pictures that show things like those you have written.

 Talk about why you write.

How We Write

 Talk about the tips for writing.

Tips for Writing

★ Think about why you are writing.

★ Think about who will read what you write.
Use words that fit your readers.

★ Print neatly and clearly.

Apply It

▶ Draw a picture showing something you would like to write and someone who might read it.

Name _____

Writing Warm-Up
Lists

We write lists so that we can read and remember things easily.

What kinds of things are on these lists? How many things are on each one?

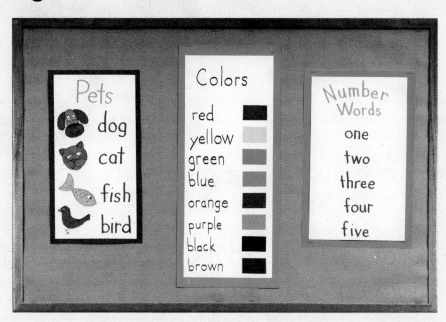

Draw or write a list of your own.

Signs

We make signs to send messages. Signs may tell rules or give directions. Signs may also tell about special times.

What does each sign tell you? How are the signs alike? How are they different?

Children's books go here.

Bake Sale Today! Room 17 10:00

Parents must stop at the office.

Draw or write to make a helpful sign for your home or classroom.

Name

Wrap-Up
Learning Together

We use listening, speaking, viewing, and writing to learn together.

What are these children doing? What tips are they following?

Apply It

Together, make a mural or poster. Show children following the tips for listening, speaking, viewing, and writing.

The Sentence

A panda sits in the bushes.

Grammar

1 What Is a Sentence?

Warm-Up Look, Listen, Talk

The dog barks.   **A cat plays.**

Try It Out • Think, Speak, Do

 Say each word group below.
Name the sentences.

 Color the picture next to each sentence.

 **1.** The girl looks.

 **2.** looks

 **3.** two fish

 **4.** Two fish swim.

Say each word group. Name the sentences.

Color each basket that has a sentence.

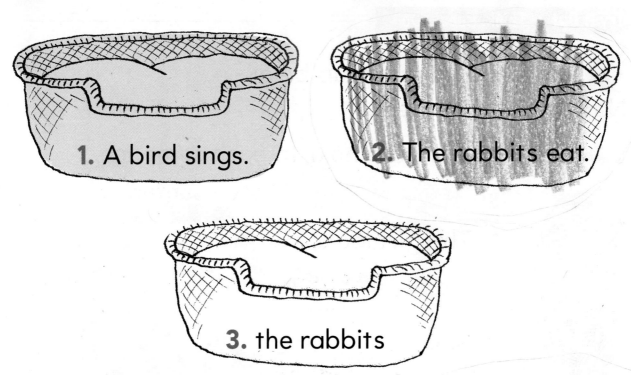

1. A bird sings.

2. The rabbits eat.

3. the rabbits

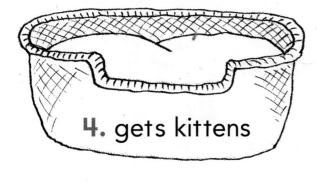

4. gets kittens

5. She gets kittens.

Grammar

2 Naming Part

Warm-Up Look, Listen, Talk

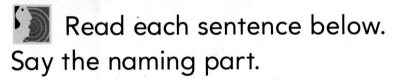

The baby sleeps. **Rusty stays home.**

Try It Out • Think, Speak, Do

Read each sentence below.
Say the naming part.

Circle the naming part in each sentence.

1. (The boys) walk.

2. Mom waves.

3. A cat looks out.

4. Birds eat food.

Find the naming part for each sentence. Say the sentences.

Draw lines to make those sentences.

The men

A woman

The bus

Two girls

People

1. _____ play.

2. _____ dig a hole.

3. _____ stops.

4. _____ step into the bus.

5. _____ sees a dress.

3 Action Part

Look, Listen, Talk

Three pigs eat.   **Bill feeds the horse.**

Try It Out • Think, Speak, Do

Read each sentence below.
Say the action part.

Circle the action part in each sentence.

1. The cow (moos).

2. Some ducks run.

3. The dog barks.

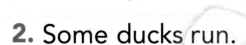

4. The kitten jumps.

Unit 1: The Sentence   **25**

 Match naming parts and action parts. Say the sentences.

Draw lines to make those sentences.

1. Dad   sleeps all day.

2. The sun   grow tall.

3. The red flowers   shines.

4. My sister   drives a truck.

5. The cat   picks the flowers.

Grammar

6 Questions

Who drives the train?   Does it go fast?

Try It Out • Think, Speak, Do

Say each sentence below. Name the questions.

Draw a line under each question.

1. Will we find a seat?

2. Many people ride to work.

3. Where are we going?

4. Is it a long ride?

5. I like trains.

Say each sentence. Name the questions.

Color the bus next to each question.

1. Who is on the bus?

2. Where are we now?

3. I see a big store.

4. What do you see?

5. This ride is fun.

Grammar / Mechanics

8 Which Kind of Sentence?

Warm-Up Look, Listen, Talk

We will eat apples.   **Will we play games?**

Try It Out • Think, Speak, Do

 Say which sentences below are correct.

 Circle the correct sentences.

1. (We need some help.)   We need some help?

2. What can I do.   What can I do?

3. When is the party?   When is the party.

4. Can you come.   Can you come?

5. It will be fun?   It will be fun.

Unit 1: The Sentence   **35**

Tell how to end each sentence.

Write the correct end mark.

1. The children worked hard ___

2. Who will come to the party ___

3. Will we have fun ___

4. What games will we play ___

5. It is time for the party ___

Question Words

Look, Listen, Talk

Use a **question word** at the beginning of a sentence that asks something.

Who	What	When	Where	Why	How

Read the questions the family asked about the rocket. Name the question word in each sentence.

Who went in the first rocket?

When did the first rocket go into space?

Where did the men sit?

Why is the door here?

How old is the rocket?

Try It Out • Think, Speak, Do

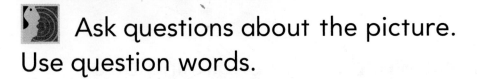 Ask questions about the picture.
Use question words.

▐▶ Circle the correct question word to begin each sentence.

1. (When   (Who)) drives the truck?

2. (What   Why) is the name of the dog?

3. (Who   Why) are the hats hard?

4. (When   What) do you wear a hat?

5. (How   Who) does water get to the fire?

6. (What   Where) do you sleep?

7. (Where   How) tall are the ladders?

 Color the fish next to each word group that is a sentence.

 **1.** The girl sees a fish.

 **2.** claps her hands

 **3.** Grandpa rows the boat.

 **4.** Grandpa smiles.

Circle the naming part in each sentence.

5. The sun shines.

6. Fish swim.

7. A boat sails by.

Circle the action part in each sentence.

8. Rob sings.

9. A child jumps.

10. Two rabbits hop.

Unit 1: The Sentence   **39**

Match naming parts and action parts.
Draw lines to make those sentences.

11. The wind   run fast.

12. Two boys   fly in the sky.

13. Kites   blows.

Circle the correct telling sentences.

14. A boy reads a book.   a boy reads a book

15. she paints   She paints.

16. This duck quacks.   this duck quacks

17. A snake hides.   a snake hides

Write the correct word to begin each
question. Write the correct end mark.

what What	

18. _____ book do you like _____

Who who	

19. _____ is your best friend _____

Can can	

20. _____ you swim _____

✏️ Circle the correct sentences.

21. Where does Sam live.   Where does Sam live?

22. Sam lives in the city.   Sam lives in the city?

23. Sam plays in the park.   Sam plays in the park?

✏️ Write the correct end mark.

24. When is lunch _____

25. Mom made soup _____

26. Soup is good for you _____

27. What is in the soup _____

28. We like the soup _____

Unit 1: The Sentence   41

Writing a Class Story

This unit also includes:

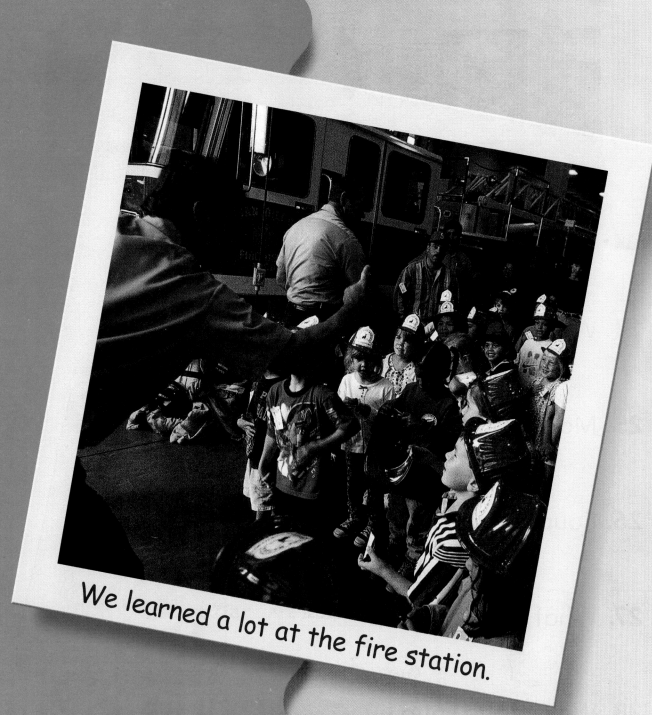

We learned a lot at the fire station.

The Writing Process

Hi! I am W.R. the Writing Star. I am going to help you learn to write. We will use **the Writing Process**.

1 PREWRITING

First, we plan our writing.

nurse

visited   today

our class

2 DRAFTING

Next, we write a draft.

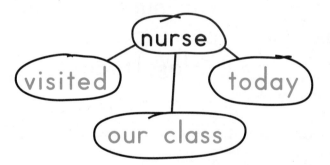

The nurse visited

our class today

Unit 2: Class Story   43

3 REVISING

Then we tell more.

school
The ∧ nurse visited

our class today

4 PROOFREADING

Next, we check and fix our writing.

school
The ∧ nurse visited

our class today.

5 PUBLISHING

Last, we copy our writing neatly and share it.

The school nurse

visited our class today.

Name

Prewriting
Choosing a Topic

The children in Ms. Hart's class wanted to write a story for their families. First, they listed their topic ideas.

Then the children talked about their ideas. They chose one to write about.

Topic Ideas

visit from police officer

(neighborhood walk)

apple picking

▶ Choose Your Topic

Who will hear or read your class story?

Draw something your class has done that your readers would like to learn about.

Make a class list of ideas. Choose one to write about.

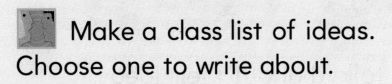

- Would you like to write about this?
- Do you remember enough about it?

Name

Exploring a Topic

The children talked about their walk. Ms. Hart wrote their details in a word web.

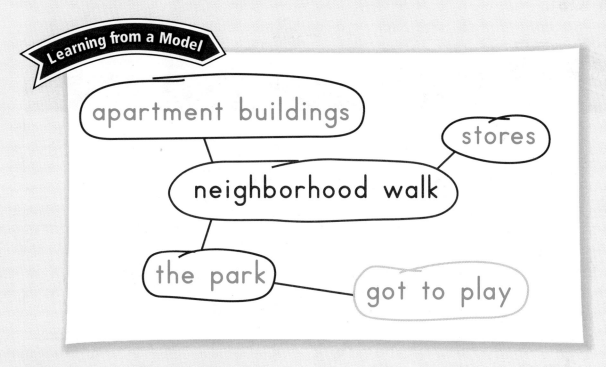

Learning from a Model

apartment buildings

stores

neighborhood walk

the park

got to play

Explore Your Topic

▶ Draw a picture about your class story idea.

Talk about your drawings. Help your teacher make a word web.

Planning a Class Story

The children looked at their word web. Then they told Ms. Hart what happened first, next, and last.

Sequence Chart

First
walked by apartment buildings
Next
passed lots of stores
Last
walked to the park and got to play

▶ Plan Your Class Story

Talk about the details in your word web. Tell your teacher what comes first, next, and last.

> Your story will be clearer if you tell what happened in order.

Name

Drafting

Drafting a Class Story

The children used their chart to help them tell their story. Ms. Hart wrote what they said. She did not worry about making mistakes.

Learning from a Model

Our class went for ~~the~~ a neighborhood walk.

First, we walked by apartment buildings. Next,

we passed lots of stores. Last, we walked to

the park and even got to play. our cheeks

were cold, but we had fun on our walk

▶ Draft Your Class Story

Choose one way to begin your class story. Tell your story to your teacher. Use your chart.

Draw a picture that shows how you felt about what happened in your story.

> Use your drawing ideas to help you end your story.

Add an ending to your class story.

Name

Revising

Revising a Class Story

Ms. Hart read the class story aloud. The children added details to tell more.

Learning from a Model

Our class went for ~~the~~ a neighborhood walk.

First, we walked by apartment buildings. Next,
food stores and toy
we passed lots of ∧ stores. Last, we walked to

the park and even got to play. our cheeks
and rosy
were cold, but we had fun on our walk
∧

▶ Revise Your Class Story

 Listen to your class story.

Draw something that you would like
to add to it.

What details
can you add
to tell more?

Tell your teacher what to write to tell more.

Name _____

Proofreading

Proofreading a Class Story

The children checked their class story for mistakes.

▶ Circle the two mistakes that they fixed.

Learning from a Model

Our class went for ~~the~~ a neighborhood walk.

First, we walked by apartment buildings. Next,
food stores and toy
we passed lots of ˄ stores. Last, we walked to

Our
the park and even got to play. ~~our~~ cheeks
and rosy
were cold, but we had fun on our walk.
˄

▶ Proofread Your Class Story

Check your class story. Together, fix any mistakes that you find.

Be sure each sentence begins with a capital letter and ends with the correct mark.

Publishing

Publishing a Class Story

The children thought of a good way to publish their class story. Ms. Hart made a neat final copy. The children made a mural to go with it.

Name

▶ Publish Your Class Story

 Think about who will hear or read your class story. Draw one special way to share it.

Talk about your drawings.

Choose one special way to share your class story.

- Do you each want to have your own copy?
- Do you want to make one big display?

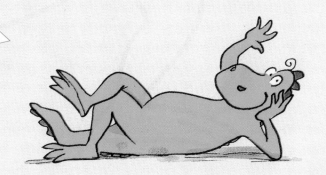

Unit 2: Class Story

55

▶ Reflect

Do what W.R. says. Then color the picture.

That was fun! You did a great job. Tell what you liked about writing your class story.

Name

Following Directions

Always listen carefully to directions so you know exactly what you need to do.

 Listen to these tips.

Listen for words such as <u>first</u>, <u>next</u>, and <u>last</u>. They will help you remember the order of the steps.

Tips for Listening to Directions

⭐ Listen to all of the directions.

⭐ Do each step in order.

⭐ Ask for help if you need it.

Apply It

 Listen to the directions for making special animals like these.

 In the first box, draw a picture of one thing you will need. Then follow the directions to make your animal in the other box.

Following Picture Directions

Pictures can show you how to do or make something. Look at this set of pictures in order. Each picture shows one step.

What does this set of pictures show how to do? What are the children doing in each picture?

Name _____

 Listen to these tips.

Tips for Following Picture Directions

★ Look at all of the pictures.

★ Follow the steps in order.

★ Do the steps one at a time.

Apply It

✂️ ✏️ Look at this set of pictures. Follow the steps to make and use a puppet.

①

②

③

④

Nouns and Pronouns

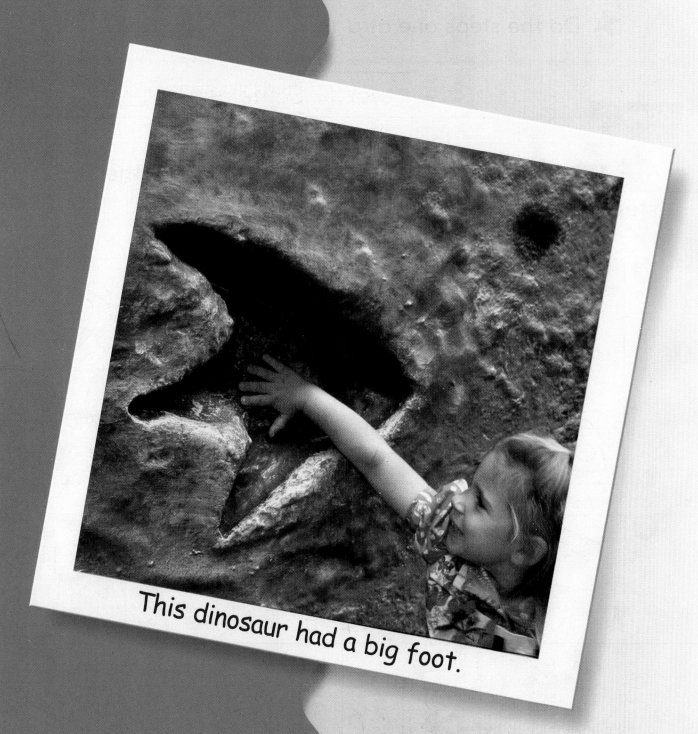

This dinosaur had a big foot.

Grammar

2 Nouns for Things and Places

Warm-Up Look, Listen, Talk

Some **nouns** name things. Some nouns name places.

The seesaw is fun.   **The children play in the park.**

Try It Out • Think, Speak, Write

Say each sentence below. Name the noun.

Draw a line under each noun.
Then write the nouns.

1. The pond is small.   _____ pond _____

2. A boat sails.   _____

3. The grass is green.   _____

4. A garden grows.   _____

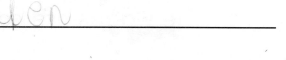

✏️▸ Look at the picture. Circle the nouns that name things and places.

sun

sand

house

deer

flower

✏️▸ Draw a line under each noun below. Then write the nouns.

1. The <u>road</u> is long. ___road_____

2. The car is red. _____

3. The sea is blue. _____

4. The beach is hot. _____

5. The woods are cool. _____

Grammar

4 One and More Than One

Warm-Up Look, Listen, Talk

Some **nouns** name one. Some nouns name more than one. An **s** means more than one.

One doll can talk. **Two dolls cannot talk.**

Try It Out • Think, Speak, Write

Say the noun for each picture.

Circle the noun for each picture below. Then write the nouns you circled.

1.  top (tops) ___tops___

2.  bat bats _____

3.  ball balls _____

4.  bear bears _____

✏️ **Look at the picture. Circle the nouns that name more than one.**

✏️ **Circle the noun for each picture below. Then write the nouns you circled.**

1. bird (birds) ___birds___

2. (frog) frogs _____

3. (tree) trees _____

4. boy (boys) _____

5. rock (rocks) _____

Grammar / Mechanics

5 Special Nouns

Warm-Up Look, Listen, Talk

Some nouns name special people. These **special nouns** begin with a capital letter.

We are having a party for T̲ina.

Try It Out • Think, Speak, Write

Say each sentence below. Tell how to begin the special noun.

Now write each special noun correctly.

Carlos

1. Will carlos take a picture?

2. My sister, maria, has balloons.

3. She will give kim a balloon.

4. Does pat like the cake?

Look at the picture. Circle the special nouns.

Draw a line under each special noun below. Then write the special nouns correctly.

1. The teacher helps <u>mike</u>.   Mike

2. My friend, sara, paints.

3. Did dan make a mask?

4. ana made a clay bird.

5. What did jay make?

6 More Special Nouns

Warm-Up Look, Listen, Talk

Some nouns name special animals and places. These **special nouns** begin with capital letters.

I have a dog named Rex.   **I go to Dale School.**

Try It Out • Think, Speak, Write

Say each sentence below. Tell how to begin the special nouns.

Now write each special noun correctly.

1. I live on bay road.  Bay Road

2. It is in newton. _____

3. My cat is called coco. _____

✏️▸ Look at the picture. Circle the special nouns.

City Zoo

Bird House

Lion Lane

hippo

family

✏️▸ Circle each special noun below.
Then write the special nouns correctly.

1. Where is snake street?

Snake Street

2. It is near seal lake.

3. The baby tiger is named tilly.

4. Can we see cubby, the baby bear?

Grammar / Usage

8 Pronouns

Warm-Up   Look, Listen, Talk

A **pronoun** can take the place of a **noun**.
He, she, it, and **they** are pronouns.

A **man** works.	**Mom** shops.	A **box** fell.	The **boys** help.
He works.	**She** shops.	**It** fell.	**They** help.

Try It Out • Think, Speak, Write

 Say each sentence below. Use **He, She, It,** or **They** to take the place of the underlined word or words.

▪ Now write the pronouns.

1. <u>Matt</u> wants an orange.

He

2. <u>Sue</u> likes grapes.

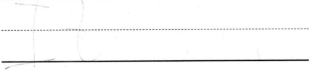

3. <u>The pears</u> are ripe.

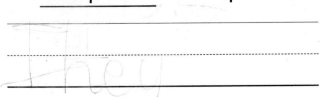

4. <u>The basket</u> is full.

Write **He**, **She**, **It**, or **They** to take the place of the underlined word or words.

1. <u>Grandma</u> makes soup.

She

2. <u>Dad</u> cuts the carrots.

_____

3. <u>Annie and Tom</u> set the table.

_____

4. <u>Polly</u> plays with a top.

_____

5. <u>The top</u> spins fast.

_____

Name _____

✏️▸ Circle the nouns that name people and animals.

1. Does a (baby) cry?   **2.** The (dog) sits down.

3. A (man) waves.   **4.** The (boy) rides a bike.

✏️▸ Circle the nouns that name things and places. Then write the nouns.

_____

5. Who is in the car?   _____

_____

6. A girl walks to school.   _____

_____

7. The girl has a new hat. _____

_____

8. Where are her books?   _____

✏️▸ Circle two nouns in each sentence.

9. Is the (duck) in the (pond?)

10. A (girl) waves a (flag.)

 Circle the noun for each picture. Then write the nouns you circled.

11. 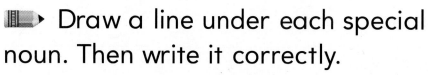 (car) cars ___car___

12. bee (bees) ___bees___

13. bird (birds) ___birds___

 Draw a line under each special noun. Then write it correctly.

14. Does cindy love her cat?

___Cindy___

15. My friend lives on north street.

___North Street___

16. This ro<u>ad</u> goes to long lake.

___Road___

17. My bird is named peep. ___Peep___

✏️▸ Write ~~the~~ words from the Word Box
to make th~~e sen~~tence correct.

I
Max

18. ___Max___ and _____ like to skate.

✏️▸ Find a pronoun from the Word Box
to take the place of each underlined
word or words. Then write the pronouns.

It
She
They
He

19. <u>Jane</u> feeds the dog.

___She_____ feeds the dog.

20. <u>The dish</u> is green.

_____ is green.

21. <u>John</u> cleans the room.

_____ cleans the room.

22. <u>Jane and John</u> are good helpers.

_____ are good helpers.

Unit 1: The Sentence

✏ Draw a line under each word group that is a sentence.

1. Tad falls down.
2. runs a race
3. my friends
4. Meg runs fast.

✏ Circle the naming part in each sentence.

5. A girl throws a ball.
6. The dog jumps up.
7. The boy rides a bike.
8. A horse trots.

✏ Circle the action part in each sentence.

9. Dad shops for food.
10. Dad holds two big bags.

✏ Draw a line under each telling sentence.

11. The man drives a truck.
12. Does he stop at the store?
13. The man lifts a box.
14. What is in the box?
15. Food is in the box.

✏▶ Draw a line under each question.

16. Where is the cat?

17. What is the cat doing?

18. The cat sits by a bush.

✏▶ Circle the correct sentences.

19. Fred sees a nest.

    Fred sees a nest?

20. Where is the nest.

    Where is the nest?

21. What is in the nest?

    What is in the nest.

22. Two birds sit in the nest.

    Two birds sit in the nest?

✏▶ Write the correct word to begin each sentence. Write the correct end mark.

23.

the
The

_____ man waves ____

24.

who
Who

_____ is that man ____

Unit 3: Nouns and Pronouns

✏️ Circle two nouns in each sentence.

25. The girl likes the beach.

26. Her sister finds a shell today.

27. The big bird sits on the sand.

28. A boy fills a pail.

✏️ Write each noun to name more than one.

29. sock _____

30. coat _____

✏️ Circle each special noun. Then write the special nouns correctly.

31. My friend, ben, is kind. _____

32. He lives on oak road. _____

33. He has a pet bird named jake. _____

Name _____

✏️▶ Write the words from the Word Box to make the sentence correct.

I
Dave

34. _____ and _____ walk to school.

✏️▶ Write a pronoun from the Word Box to take the place of the underlined words.

He	She	It	They

35. A man waits for the bus. _____

36. The bus stops. _____

37. Lynn and Pete get off the bus. _____

38. A girl waves. _____

Writing a Personal Narrative

This unit also includes:

Special Focus on Narrating
Writing a Friendly Letter
Page 108

Communication Links
Telling a Story About Yourself
Page 114

Having a Discussion
Page 116

My walk with Grandpa was lots of fun.

Name

Listening to a Personal Narrative

"A Very Special Day" is a young boy's story about himself. What one event does Pablo tell about?

Text copyright ©1994 by Pat Mora. Illustrations copyright ©1994 by Cecily Lang. Reprinted with the permission of Simon & Schuster Books for Young Readers, an imprint of Simon & Schuster Children's Publishing Division.

A Very Special Day

adapted from <u>Pablo's Tree</u>, by Pat Mora

"I'm ready, Mamá!" I say. "I'm ready for my birthday visit to Lito's. Hurry, Mamá! I want to see my tree."

I wonder if Lito, my grandfather, remembered. I wonder if he remembered to decorate my tree.

I ask, "Mamá, did Abuelito decorate my tree?"

See www.eduplace.com/kids/ for information about Pat Mora.

"Your grandfather does not forget to decorate your tree, Pablo. Do you have your suitcase? What new birthday toys are you taking to Abuelito's?" asks Mamá.

"I've got my purple car, my book about whales, my tambourine, and my flute," I say.

Every year I spend the night after my birthday at my grandfather's house. We sit under my tree. We play with my new toys. Every year Lito decorates my tree for my birthday visit. Maybe my grandfather forgot.

Name

"Are you sure he didn't forget?" I ask.

"I'm sure," says Mamá.

"Please tell me, Mamá," I say. "Tell me what Lito put on my tree. Is it lights? Is it little *piñatas*?"

Mamá smiles. "Pablo," she says, "don't you like surprises? Come. Let's go see your tree."

As we drive along I ask, "Is it little animals? Is it candy?" My mother just smiles and winks.

"Lito! Lito!" I say. "I'm here! I'm here!"

Lito opens the screen door. His face is happy,
like a full moon. Lito gives my mother a kiss and
a hug.

"Lito," I say, "I brought my new birthday toys. We
can sit under my tree and play with my toys all day
and all night."

Name

Lito and my mother laugh.

"Pablo," says Lito, hugging me, "*¿Cómo está mi nieto grande?* How is my big grandson?"

I give Lito a giant hug. He almost falls down.

"Pablo!" says Mamá. "*Cuidado*. Be careful." But
Lito likes my giant hugs.

"Let's go see my tree," I say. "Hurry. Hurry, Lito."
I take Lito's hand and pull him to the back door.

Name

When I see my tree, I run to it. I touch the tiny colored bells and wind chimes. "Ooooh," I say. I run around the tree, touching the bells and chimes. The wind blows and my tree jingles and rings.

I give Lito another giant hug, and again I almost knock him down. But he just smiles.

Listening As a Writer

Think About the Personal Narrative

 Circle the picture that shows what Pablo told about in his story.

 Circle the word that Pablo used to tell about himself.

I   she   you

 Circle the picture that shows what Pablo's grandfather put on the tree this year.

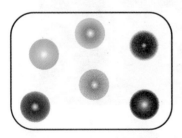  

Responding

Draw the part of the story that you liked best.

What Makes a Great Personal Narrative?

A true story about yourself is called a **personal narrative**. It tells about something that really happened to you.

When you write a story about yourself, remember to do these things.

★ Use I and me.

★ Use details that tell who, what, where, and when.

★ Write what happened in order.

GRAMMAR CHECK

Begin each special name with a capital letter.

FINAL COPY

Listen to Katrice's story about herself and what W.R. said about it.

Katrice Willis

> My Caterpillar
> by Katrice Willis
> One day I found a striped caterpillar on a low tree branch. I brought the caterpillar home and kept it warm. A few days later it made a sticky cocoon. Then the caterpillar slept for a while. After two weeks, it turned into a beautiful butterfly. It had orange and black wings. The butterfly was a new pet. I felt sad when I let it go. That's why I will never catch a caterpillar again.

> You used I to tell about yourself.

> These are good details.

> Good! You told the events in order.

Listening As a Writer

Talk with your classmates.

- What one event did Katrice tell about?
- What happened first in Katrice's story? What happened next? What happened last?

See www.eduplace.com/kids/hme/ for more examples of student writing.

Name _____

Write a Personal Narrative

▶ Think About Topics

▬▶ Draw a picture to answer each question below.

When did you help someone?

When were you surprised?

When did you learn something?

▶ Choose Your Topic

 Talk about your drawings and ideas.

Circle the drawing on page 97 that you will write about.

Finish these sentences.

I will write about _____

_____.

I will write my story for _____

_____ to read.

Name _____

Using Details

Give your readers a clear picture. Use lots of **details** in your story. The words <u>who</u>, <u>what</u>, <u>where</u>, and <u>when</u> will help you think of details.

Which picture and sentence below give more details?

It had wings.

It had orange and black wings.

Try It Together

Color the house and add details to it.

Talk with your class about the details you added. Say a sentence about the house.

Unit 4: Personal Narrative   **99**

Explore and Plan Your Personal Narrative

Draw pictures and details in the three boxes. Show what happened first, next, and last.

Then write details under each drawing.

> Draw and write details that tell **who, what, where,** and **when**.

First

See www.eduplace.com/kids/hme/ for graphic organizers.

Name

Next

Draw and write details about what happened **next**.

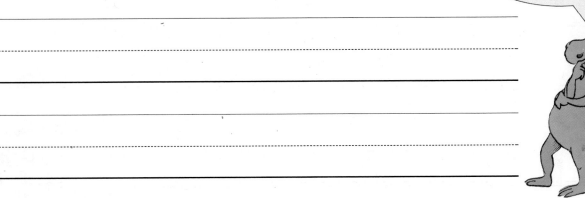

Unit 4: Personal Narrative   **101**

▶ **Explore and Plan** continued

Last

Draw and write details about what happened **last**.

Name _____

▶ Write Your Personal Narrative

 Tell your story, using your drawings.

 Write your story. Write what happened first, next, and last. Use your drawings and details.

> Include lots of details to help your readers picture what happened.

Unit 4: Personal Narrative   **103** ▷

Revise Your Personal Narrative

Look at this sentence. What words did Katrice add to tell more?

striped

One day I found a ∧ caterpillar

low

on a ∧ tree branch.

Revise each sentence below. Add a word from the Word Box to tell more. Use a ∧.

pine   sleepy

1. My cat naps.

2. I saw the tree.

Read your story to someone. Talk about where you can add details.

Add details to your story to tell more.

Name

▶ Proofread Your Personal Narrative

Look at these sentences.
How did Katrice fix the mistakes?

> The
> ~~the~~ butterfly was a new pet. I
> I
> felt sad when ~~i~~ let it go~~?~~.

▮▶ Find mistakes with capital letters and end marks. Fix two mistakes in each sentence.

1. bob and i saw the bike.

2. was it the red bike

Proofread your story.
Fix mistakes that you find.

Begin each special name with a capital letter.

Unit 4: Personal Narrative **105**

Publish Your Personal Narrative

Make a neat final copy of your story. Write a title.

Share your story. Here are some ideas.

> Be sure you wrote all of your letters correctly and used good spacing.

Reflect

Write what you like best about your story.

I like _____

_____

_____

 Tech Tip If you wrote your story on a computer, leave room on each page to add pictures.

Name

 Writing Prompts

Use these ideas to write stories about yourself. Write details that your readers will want to know.

1 **PHYSICAL EDUCATION**

Write about a time you learned to play a sport or a game. Who helped you? What happened?

2 **SOCIAL STUDIES**

Write about a time you had fun on a holiday. Where were you? Who was there? What did you do?

3 **ART**

Write about a time you made something special for someone. What happened when you gave it to the person? How did you feel?

See www.eduplace.com/kids/hme/ for more prompts.

Writing a Friendly Letter

Juan wrote a **friendly letter** to Ling.

Listen to Juan's letter and what W.R. said about it.

Good start!
This names the person you are writing to.

This part of your letter has details.

Dear Ling,

My family went to a huge water park. It was a lot of fun. The water slide was so high my heart jumped!

This is where you sign your name.

Your friend,
Juan

Listening As a Writer

✏ Circle the picture that shows who got the letter.

Juan

Ling

✏ Circle the picture that shows who wrote the letter.

Juan

Ling

✏ Circle the picture that shows what the letter is about.

✏ Circle the word that tells where Juan wrote his name on the letter.

top   bottom   middle

How to Write a Friendly Letter

Make a plan before you write your letter.

▪▬▸ Draw the person you will write to.

▪▮▸ Write the person's name.

▪▬▸ Draw a picture of what you will write about.

▪▮▸ Think about your drawings. Then write your letter.

Dear _____,

_____,

Name

 Look at this envelope. What did Juan write on it?

Juan Arias
8 Crow Lane
Salem, NC   27103

 This is Juan's **return address**.

Juan put a **postage stamp** here.

Juan sent his letter to Ling at this **mailing address**.

Ling Chen
2 Leaf Street
Chicago, IL   60626

✏ Write your return address.

_____

_____

_____

_____

_____

_____

✏ Address an envelope and mail your letter.

Telling a Story About Yourself

Ellen told a story about herself.

Listen to her story. Look at the pictures.

1 I **love** to go fishing!

2 My dad and I went to the ocean. I caught a **huge** fish!

3 Dad helped me reel it in. It was **very** slippery. We looked at its fins.

4 Then we let the fish go. I wish I could go fishing every day!

How did Ellen use her voice as she told her story? How did she use her face and hands?

Name _____

Listen to these tips.

Tips for Telling a Story About Yourself

★ Look at your listeners.

★ Use your face and hands.

★ Speak clearly. Be sure everyone can hear you.

Apply It _____

Think of a story you can tell about yourself. Draw a picture of yourself telling your story.

 Follow the tips as you tell your story.

Having a Discussion

These children are talking together.

 Look at the picture. Listen to what they say.

What are the children in the picture talking about? What is each child saying and doing?

Listen to these tips.

Tips for Having a Discussion

Make sure you ask questions to find out more.

⭐ Take turns.

⭐ Speak clearly. Be sure everyone can hear you.

⭐ Listen carefully to what others say.

Apply It

Talk with your group. Choose colors for this class flag.

Now color the flag. Use the colors that your group chose.

Verbs

The children run with the kite.

Grammar / Usage

6 **was** and **were**

Use **was** in a sentence with a **noun** that names one. Use **were** in a sentence with a **noun** that names more than one.

One bird was in the nest.
Two birds were out of the nest.

Try It Out • Think, Speak, Write

 Say each sentence below. Use the correct verb.

✏ Circle the correct verb to finish each sentence. Then write those verbs.

1. **was** (circled)
    were
    The storm ___was___ over.

2. **was**
    were
    The boys ___were___ cold.

3. **was**
    were
    Mom ___was___ at home.

▸ Circle the correct verbs in Beth's poem.

Snowy Night

1. The flakes (was ⟨were⟩) light.

2. The trees (was ⟨were⟩) white.

3. The moon (⟨was⟩ were) bright.

4. The stars (⟨was⟩ were) out tonight.

▸ Now write the verbs you circled.

1. ___were___

2. _____

3. _____

4. _____

▸ Write **was** or **were** to finish each sentence.

5. My house _____ nice and warm.

6. The windows _____ frosty.

Words That Look the Same

Look, Listen, Talk

Find words in the picture that are spelled the same. Use each word in a sentence to tell about the picture.

row

bark

bark

row

Some words are spelled the same but have different meanings.

bark	the sound a dog makes
bark	the thick skin of a tree

Look at the pictures and words below. Tell two meanings for the word **bat**.

bat

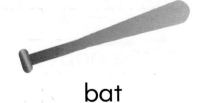

bat

Apply It

Find the sentence with the underlined word that means the same as the picture. Circle that sentence.

1. Dad writes with a <u>pen</u>.

2. The sheep are in the <u>pen</u>.

3. Planes <u>fly</u> in the air.

4. A <u>fly</u> is on my hand.

5. Jon will <u>ring</u> the bell.

6. Mom wears a <u>ring</u> on her hand.

7. I found a <u>rock</u> in the dirt.

8. I <u>rock</u> the baby to sleep.

Name _____

Name _____

✏️➤ Write the contractions for t... ...erlined words.

19. That book <u>is</u> <u>not</u> mine. _____

20. I <u>cannot</u> find my book. _____

21. I <u>do</u> <u>not</u> have time to look. _____

Mixed Review 22–26.

✏️➤ Circle the correct verb or contraction to finish each sentence in this part of Rosa's letter.

Dear Uncle Marco,

My new bike (are is) green.

I (can't isn't) ride the bike.

Mom (helps helped) me yesterday.

My dad (help helps) me today.

He (runs run) beside me.

Cumulative Review

Unit 1: The Sentence

 Circle each word group that is a sentence.

1. a green frog
2. The little frog jumps.
3. Bees buzz.
4. live in a hive

Circle the naming part in each sentence.
Draw a line under each action part.

5. A big bear sleeps.

6. One cub plays.

7. Lee takes a picture.

Write the correct word to begin
each sentence. Write the correct end mark.

8.
| where |
| Where |

_____ is the snake ___

9.
| birds |
| Birds |

_____ fly in the sky ___

10.
| the |
| The |

_____ cat runs fast ___

11.
| who |
| Who |

_____ sees a bug ___

138   Cumulative Review

Copyright © Houghton Mifflin Company. All rights reserved.

Listening to a Story

"A New House" is a story about two little animals. What problem does one of them have?

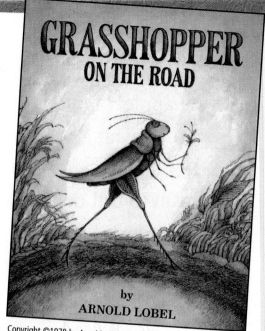

Copyright ©1978 by Arnold Lobel. Reprinted by permission of HarperCollins Publishers.

A New House

from <u>Grasshopper on the Road,</u> by Arnold Lobel

Grasshopper wanted to go on a journey. "I will find a road," he said. "I will follow that road wherever it goes."

One morning Grasshopper found a road. . . . The road went up a steep hill. Grasshopper climbed to the top. He found a large apple lying on the ground.

"I will have my lunch," said Grasshopper. He ate a big bite of the apple.

See www.eduplace.com/kids/ for information about Arnold Lobel.

"Look what you did!" said a worm, who lived in the apple. "You have made a hole in my roof! It is not polite to eat a person's house," said the worm.

"I am sorry," said Grasshopper. Just then the apple began to roll down the road on the other side of the hill.

Name

"Stop me! Catch me!" cried the worm.
The apple was rolling faster and faster.

"Help, my head is bumping on the walls! My dishes
are falling off the shelf!" cried the worm.

Grasshopper ran after the apple.

"Everything is a mess in here!" cried the worm.
"My bathtub is in the living room. My bed is in the
kitchen!"

Grasshopper kept running down the hill. But he could not catch the apple.

"I am getting dizzy," cried the worm. "My floor is on the ceiling! My attic is in the cellar!"

The apple rolled and rolled. It rolled all the way down to the bottom of the hill. The apple hit a tree. It smashed into a hundred pieces.

"Too bad, worm," said Grasshopper. "Your house is gone."

Name _____

The worm climbed up the side of the tree.

"Oh, never mind," said the worm. "It was old, and it had a big bite in it anyway. This is a fine time for me to find a new house."

Grasshopper looked up into the tree. He saw that it was filled with apples.

Grasshopper smiled, and he went on down the road.

Name

Listening As a Writer

Think About the Story

 Circle the two characters from the story.

 Circle the problem from the story.

Responding

Draw the animal from the story that you liked better.

What Makes a Great Story?

A **story** has make-believe characters. It tells about a problem they solve.

When you write your story, remember to do these things.

★ Tell what happens at the beginning, in the middle, and at the end of your story.

★ Write details about the characters. They are the people or animals in the story.

★ Write about a problem that the characters solve.

GRAMMAR CHECK

Make sure that you use <u>is</u>, <u>are</u>, <u>was</u>, and <u>were</u> correctly.

FINAL COPY

Listen to Kristin's story and what W.R. said about it.

Kristin Roe

The Friendly Tadpole
by Kristin Roe
Once there was a friendly tadpole named Lily. Lily was small, but she liked to play in the big pond.

One day Lily asked the other tadpoles to play. They said, "No, we already have friends." Lily was sad.

The next day, another tadpole and his mother moved into the pond. His name was Tad. Lily said, "Hello, welcome to the pond."

> You wrote good details about Lily.

> Writing your character's exact words makes your story more interesting.

See www.eduplace.com/kids/hme/ for more examples of student writing.

Unit 6: Story

151

> She asked Tad if he would like to play. He said, "Yes." Lily and Tad had lots of fun in the pond. They played tag and had races. Lily and Tad became best friends.

Your story has a clear beginning, middle, and end.

Listening As a Writer

 Talk with your classmates.

- Who are the characters in Kristin's story?
- What problem does one character have?
- How is the problem solved?

Name _____

Story Characters

Characters are the people or animals in a story. They are make-believe, but they may talk and act like they are real.

I help my friends.

Try It Together

 Choose a character from above. Draw a picture of the character doing what it likes to do best.

Tell your class about your drawing.

Choose a Character

Who will read your story? Talk about characters your readers might like.

Draw the character you will write about.

Write your character's name. Write details that tell what the character is like.

Name _____

Name _____

Beginning, Middle, End

The **beginning** of a story tells who the characters are and where the story takes place. The **middle** tells about a problem. The **end** tells how the problem is solved.

Beginning

Middle

End

Try It Together

➡ Draw a different ending for the story above.

 Tell your class about your drawing.

Explore and Plan Your Story

What problem will your character need to solve?

Draw your main character and where the story will take place.

Draw pictures in the three boxes. Show what will happen at the beginning, in the middle, and at the end of your story.

Write details under each drawing.

Beginning

See www.eduplace.com/kids/hme/ for graphic organizers.

Name

Middle

Draw the story problem.

Explore and Plan continued

Draw how the problem is solved.

End

Name _____

▶ Write Your Story

A good story has an interesting beginning. Which of these beginnings is more interesting?

| This is about a pig. | A big pink pig rolled happily in the mud. |

Think of a good beginning and then tell your story. Use your drawings and details.

Write an interesting beginning for your story. Then write the rest of the story.

Look at your drawings and details as you write your draft.

Revise Your Story

What changes did Kristin
make in this sentence to tell more?

> Once there was a friendly
> ~~tadpole~~ named Lily
> baby frog.
> ^   ^

Change a word and add a word in each
sentence to tell more. Use words from the box
and a ∧.

shaggy	hopped	poodle	green

1. The frog moved.

2. The dog ran.

Have a writing conference like the one
on the next page.

Think about what your classmate said.
Make changes to your story.

Having a Writing Conference

 **What are these children saying and doing?**

Before you share your story, write a question about a part you want help with.

1. Will you listen to my story?

   Sure!

2. I liked your story. You told about funny things the cat did and where it went at the end of the story.

3. Did I tell enough about what the cat did?

   Yes, but where did the cat come from?

4. Thanks for all of your help.

   Thanks for sharing your story with me!

▶ Proofread Your Story

What mistakes did Kristin find in this sentence? How did she fix them?

> Tad   like
> She asked ~~tad~~ if he would ~~lik~~ to play.

▶ Find mistakes with capital letters, end marks, spelling, and using verbs correctly. Fix two mistakes in each sentence. Use words from the box.

bloom
blue
is
were

1. The kite are blu.

2. Does nina like it

Proofread your story.
Use the Proofreading Checklist.

Did you use <u>is</u>, <u>are</u>, <u>was</u>, and <u>were</u> correctly?

Proofreading Checklist

☐ capital letters
☐ end marks
☐ spelling

Name _____

Publish Your Story

Make a neat final copy of your story. Write a title.

Look at Ideas for Sharing on the next page. Share your story.

Reflect

What do you like about your story?

_____

I like _____

_____

_____

_____

_____

_____

_____.

Tech Tip Save your story before you turn off the computer.

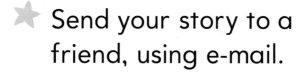

Ideas for Sharing

Write It

⭐ Send your story to a friend, using e-mail.

Say It

⭐ Read your story aloud as some classmates act it out.

Show It

⭐ Draw pictures and make a cover for your story. Put the pages together to make a book.

Where is Andy?

Name _____

 # Writing Prompts

Use these ideas to write stories. Write a clear beginning, middle, and end. Think about who will read your story.

1 **FINE ART**

How did this apple get so big? How did it get into the room? Write a funny story about the apple.

The Listening Room (La Chambre d'écoute) 1958, René Magritte 1898-1967

2 **PHYSICAL EDUCATION**

Write a story telling how a character wins a race. Who is your character? What kind of race is it?

3 **READING**

Write a story about meeting your favorite book character. How did you meet? What did you do?

 See www.eduplace.com/kids/hme/ for more prompts.

Writing a Book Report

Nicole wrote a **book report**.

 Listen to Nicole's book report and what W.R. said about it.

> The title is the name of the book.

Title   <u>Shoes Like Miss Alice's</u>
Author   <u>Angela Johnson</u>

> The author is the person who wrote the book.

This book is about <u>Miss Alice and how she takes care of Sara. They dance together. They eat together. Miss Alice and Sara go for a walk.</u>

> Good! You told what happened in the book.

I like this book because <u>Miss Alice is nice to Sara. Miss Alice has shoes for every different thing she does. She makes me smile.</u>

> You told how you feel about the book.

Listening As a Writer

✏️ Circle the title of the book that Nicole wrote about.

<u>Shoes Like Miss Alice's</u>   <u>Lots of Shoes</u>

✏️ Circle the name of the book's author.

Miss Alice   Angela Johnson

✏️ Circle the picture that shows what the book is about.

✏️ Circle the picture that shows how Nicole felt about the book.

How to Write a Book Report

Choose a book that you know and like.

▪️➤ Draw a character from the book.

▪️➤ Write the character's name.

_____

_____

▪️➤ Draw something that happens in the book.

▪️➤ Write a sentence about your drawing.

_____

_____

_____

Write your book report.

Draw a line under the title of the book.

Title _____

Author _____

This book is about _____

_____

_____

_____ .

I like this book because _____

_____

_____

_____ .

Viewing Story Pictures

Pictures can help you understand a story.

Listen as your teacher reads the story again. Look at each picture.

What new things did you learn by looking at the pictures?

Listen to these tips.

Tips for Viewing Story Pictures

★ Listen to the words of the story.

★ Look at the pictures.

★ Think about new things that the pictures show you.

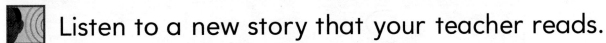

Apply It

 Listen to a new story that your teacher reads.

▬▶ Draw two pictures for the story.

 Share and talk about your pictures.

Adjectives

The furry lion roars at the tiny butterfly.

1 Adjectives: How Things Look

I Went Walking

WRITTEN BY
Sue Williams

ILLUSTRATED BY
Julie Vivas

Read the sentence. Say the word that tells about the horse.

I saw a brown horse looking at me.

—from I Went Walking, by Sue Williams

Some words tell how things look. These words are called **adjectives**.

The **big** cow moos.   A **round** pig eats.
The **yellow** sun shines.   I picked **three** flowers.

Try It Out • Think, Speak, Write

🔊 Say each sentence below. Name the adjective.

✏️ Draw a line under each adjective. Then write those adjectives.

1. The <u>two</u> frogs sit.

two

2. A <u>spotted</u> dog looks.

spotted

3. A <u>little</u> bee flies by.

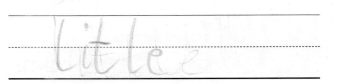
little

4. The <u>fat</u> cat purrs.

fat

✏ **1–4.** Read Lee's news story. Circle three more adjectives.

Pet Show

The first grade class had a pet show on Friday.

1. Ben brought a (tan) bunny.

2. Nina brought (four) turtles.

3. Cam brought a (long) snake.

4. Jen brought a (little) mouse.

✏ Now write the adjectives you circled.

1. __tan__   2. __four__

3. __long__   4. __little__

✏ Finish this sentence. Write an adjective that tells how the hamster looks.

5. Greg brought a ___fat___ hamster.

2 Adjectives: Taste and Smell

One-Minute Warm-Up

Frog and Toad All Year
Arnold Lobel

Read the sentences. Say the words that tell about the ice cream.

"I wish we had some sweet, cold ice cream," said Frog.
"What a good idea," said Toad.

—from "Ice Cream" in <u>Frog and Toad All Year</u>, by Arnold Lobel

Some **adjectives** tell how things taste or smell.

The nuts taste salty.   **The flower smells sweet.**

Try It Out • Think, Speak, Write

🔊 Say each sentence below. Name the adjective.

✏️ Draw a line under each adjective. Then write those adjectives.

1. The air smells <u>fresh</u>.

fresh

2. I like <u>sour</u> pickles.

sour

3. The ham tastes <u>spicy</u>.

spicy

4. I want a <u>sweet</u> apple.

sweet

1–4. Read Mandy's recipe. Circle three more adjectives.

Silly Stew

1. First, I put (salty) chips in a pot.

2. Next, I add sweet jelly.

3. Last, I mix in sour milk.

4. My stew smells (fishy)!

Now write the adjectives you circled.

1. salty

2. sweet

3. sour

4. fishy

Think and Write

Write an adjective to finish each sentence.

5. This stew tastes sweet.

6. That cake smells sweet.

Grammar / Usage

4 Adjectives with <u>er</u> and <u>est</u>

One-Minute Warm-Up

Look at the brushes. Say sentences that tell how the brushes are different.

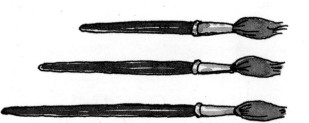

Add **er** to **adjectives** to compare two.
Add **est** to compare more than two.

| small | smaller | smallest |

Try It Out • Think, Speak, Write

 Finish each sentence. Use the adjectives from the Word Box.

Now write the adjectives.

Tim   Max   Fred

1. Tim is _tall_____.

| tallest |
| tall |
| taller |

2. Max is _____ than Tim.

3. Fred is the _____ of all.

1–3. Proofread Amy's letter. Fix two more mistakes in using **er** and **est**.

Now write the letter correctly.

Proofreading

Dear Pen Pal,

I have a sister and a brother. I am the
oldest
~~older~~ child in my family. Pete is oldest

than Beth. He is a fast runner. I am the

faster of all.

Your friend,
Amy

Think and Write

Finish each sentence. Use an adjective
that ends with **er** or **est**.

4. Amy is _____ than Pete.

5. Amy is the _____ one of all.

✏️▶ Draw a line under each adjective that tells how something looks. Then write the adjectives.

1. The fish live in a <u>square</u> tank. _____ *square*

2. The <u>red</u> fish chase each other. _____ *red*

3. A fish hides by a <u>tall</u> plant. _____ *tall*

4. <u>Two</u> snails are in the tank. _____ *Two*

✏️▶ Circle three adjectives in the Word Box that name the colors in this flag. Then write those adjectives in the sentence.

pink	(red)	(blue)	black	(white)	green

5–7. The flag is _____ *red* _____,

_____ *white* _____, and _____ *blue* _____.

Unit 7: Adjectives   **183** ▶

Write each sentence. Then draw a line under the adjective that tells how something tastes or smells.

8. The corn tastes sweet.

The corn tastes sweet.

9. The fire smells smoky.

The fire smells smoky

Draw a line under each adjective that tells how something feels or sounds. Then write the adjectives.

10. The music is loud. ___loud___

11. Ed sits on a hard chair. ___hard___

12. A cat sleeps on a soft pillow. ___soft___

13. Ed hears a buzzing sound. ___buzzing___

▶ Write the adjective **fast**, **faster**, or **fastest** to finish each sentence.

14. A bike is _____ .

15. A car is _____ than a bike.

16. A plane is the _____ way to go.

Mixed Review 17–20.

▶ Read Anna's diary page. Circle the adjective that finishes each sentence.

What was in the (big   loud) box?

A (gray   salty) cat was inside.

This cat is (smallest   smaller) than my cat.

This cat has (sweet   thick) fur.

Unit 1: The Sentence

✏️▶ Circle the naming part in each sentence.
Draw a line under each action part.

1. The children play in the snow.

2. The girl sits.

3. Mom pulls the sled.

✏️▶ Write the two telling sentences.

Who has a pet?	Meg has a cat.
The cat purrs.	Is it a good pet?

4. _____

5. _____

✏️▶ Write each sentence correctly.

SHOW TODAY

6. where is the show

_____

7. the twins will sing

_____

Name

Listening to a Description

In this description, what words does the writer use to help you see, hear, and feel winter?

Text copyright © 1990 by Ron Hirschi. Photographs copyright © 1990 by Thomas D. Mangelsen. Reprinted by permission of Penguin Putnam Inc.

A Winter Day

from Winter, by Ron Hirschi

Winter is
an icy morning
when all is calm.
All is silent
beneath the deep snow,
inside the marmot's burrow,
and inside the bear's
snug den.

Black-capped chickadee

Outside,
the icy branches glisten
while chickadees
search for beetles,
spiders, and caterpillars
that hide in
their cocoons.

This is the season
for ptarmigan
to hide in feathers
of white,
for deer to leap through
the crunching snow,
and for geese to wander
far to the south.

Willow ptarmigan

Name _____

Reading As a Writer

Think About the Description

✏️▸ Circle two words the writer used to help you see or feel winter.

icy   den   calm   bear

✏️▸ Circle the word the writer used to help you hear the sound of deer on the snow.

calm   crunching   snug

✏️▸ Write the word from page 192 that tells what

_____

_____

the icy tree branches do. _____

Responding

✏️▸ Draw what winter is like where you live.

[blank box]

📝 Write words that tell what winter looks, sounds, feels, tastes, or smells like where you live.

Unit 8: Description   **193**

What Makes a Great Description?

A **description** tells how something looks, sounds, smells, tastes, and feels.

When you write a description, remember to do these things.

★ Write about one place or thing.

★ Begin with a topic sentence that names what you will describe.

★ Use words that tell how your topic looks, sounds, smells, tastes, and feels.

GRAMMAR CHECK

- Add **er** to most adjectives to compare two things.
- Add **est** to most adjectives to compare more than two things.

194   A Published Model

Name _____

Student Model

FINAL COPY

Listen to Jhogel's description and what W.R. said about it.

Jhogel Florentino

The Beach

by Jhogel Florentino

I like to go to the beach in the summer. The sun is so bright that I wear sunglasses. It seems brighter than at home. Birds make music. The sand feels hot on my feet. The water is as cold as ice cubes. It tastes salty. I really like going to the beach.

> You name the place you are writing about in your first sentence. Good!

> Comparing the water to ice cubes lets me know <u>how</u> cold it feels. Brrr!

Reading As a Writer

 Talk with your classmates.

- Which words did Jhogel use to tell how things looked, felt, or tasted?
- What did he mean when he wrote that the birds make music?

See www.eduplace.com/kids/hme/ for more examples of student writing.

Unit 8: Description   **195**

Write a Description

▶ **Choose Your Topic**

✏️▶ Draw a thing and a place that you can describe well.

thing

place

🗨 Talk about your drawings. Which one can you describe better?

✏️▶ Finish these sentences.

I will describe _____.

I will write my paper for _____ to read.

Name

Using Your Senses

You use your **senses** to see, hear, smell, taste, and feel things. Some words describe what you learn when you use your senses.

red —————— juicy

crunchy —————— bumpy

Try It Together

 Think about this dog. Say words that tell how it looks, feels, sounds, and smells.

 Write your words next to the pictures below.

 _____

 _____

Unit 8: Description   **197**

Explore and Plan Your Description

Think about your topic. Say words that tell how it looks, sounds, smells, tastes, and feels.

Write words that describe your topic.

Five Senses Chart

My topic is _____.

	See	
	Hear	
	Smell	
	Taste	
	Touch	

Number your details in the order you want to write about them.

See www.eduplace.com/kids/hme/ for graphic organizers.

Name _____

Focus Skill

Topic Sentences

A **topic sentence** tells what you are writing about. What is the topic of Jhogel's description?

I like to go to the beach in the summer.

Try It Together

Think about the pictures. Say two topic sentences for each one.

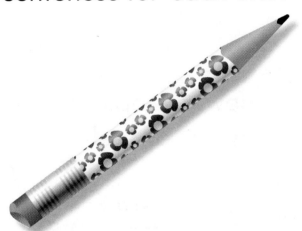

Write Your Description

Write a topic sentence for your description. Then write the rest of your paper.

Use your Five Senses Chart as you write.

Unit 8: Description   **199**

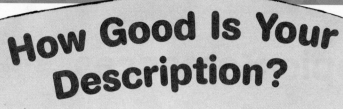
How Good Is Your Description?

 Color the star beside each sentence that tells about your writing.

 I wrote about one place or thing.

 My topic sentence names what I described.

 I used words that tell how my topic looks, sounds, smells, tastes, or feels.

I used what I have learned about capital letters, end marks, spelling, and using words correctly.

Be a writing star like W.R.!

200   Revising

Name _____

Revise Your Description

 What changes did Jhogel make? Why?

The sun is so bright that I wear sunglasses. Birds make ~~noises.~~ ^{music} It seems brighter than at home. The sand ~~is~~ ^{feels} ^{on my feet} hot.

Use words from the box and a ∧ to add words and change two words. Move a sentence that is out of order.

glows	on the sides

My sneakers have blue and purple stripes. A silver patch shows up in the dark. The laces are purple too.

 Have a writing conference. See page 202.

Make changes to your writing. Can you color all the stars on page 200 now?

Unit 8: Description   **201**

Having a Writing Conference

What are these children saying and doing?

After you listen to a classmate's writing, first tell what you liked about it.

1
Will you listen to my description?

Yes, I would really like to hear it.

2
I liked your topic sentence. You remembered to write about only one topic.

3
How can I make this part clearer?

You could add words that tell what it sounds like and feels like.

4
Thanks for helping me with my description.

You are welcome. I think you did a great job!

Name

Proofread Your Description

What do you look for and do when you proofread? How can you use the Proofreading Checklist and Proofreading Marks to help you?

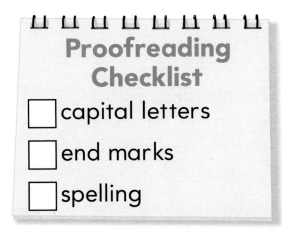

Proofreading Checklist

☐ capital letters

☐ end marks

☐ spelling

Mark each box on the checklist as you proofread your writing.

Proofreading Marks

ℐ take out

≡ capital letter

▶ Practice proofreading on page 204 before you proofread your own writing.

Proofread your description. Use the Proofreading Checklist and Proofreading Marks.

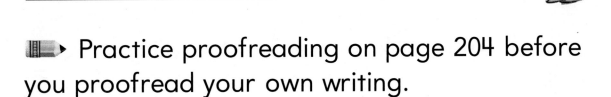

- Add **er** to most adjectives to compare two things.
- Add **est** to most adjectives to compare more than two things.

Unit 8: Description   **203**

Proofreading Practice

 How did the writer fix these mistakes?

is this book ~~newest~~ newer than that one.?

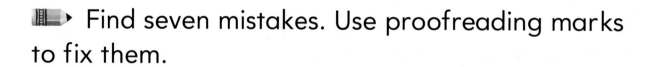 Find two mistakes in each sentence. Use proofreading marks to fix them.

Fix mistakes with capital letters, end marks, spelling, and using words.

1. Grapes ar a good snack

2. I think they taste sweetest than oranges?

3. My pal jeff. Likes bananas better.

Find seven mistakes. Use proofreading marks to fix them.

popcorn is my favorite snack It smells

sweetest and buttery when Dad and I cook it?

popcorn crunches when I eat it. i like popcorn

better thn any other snack!

Name _____

Publish Your Description

Make a neat final copy of your paper. Write a title.

Be sure you wrote all letters correctly and used good spacing.

Look at Ideas for Sharing on the next page. Share your writing.

Reflect

▸ Write what you like best about your description.

_____

I like _____

_____

_____.

▸ What would you like to do the next time you write?

_____

I want to _____.

Tech Tip Use the shift key to make capital letters.

Unit 8: Description   **205**

Ideas for Sharing

Write It

⭐ Use a computer to write your paper. Use special lettering for the title.

Say It

⭐ Read your paper aloud in the Author's Chair.

Show It

⭐ Share your paper with your family. Have someone write nice things about it. Share what they write with your class.

Name _____

✓ Writing Prompts

Use these ideas to write descriptions. Think about who will read your description.

1

ART

Look at the people in this park. Write a description telling what they see, hear, smell, and feel.

City Park, 1992. Oil on Canvas,
Anna Belle Lee Washington b. 1924, Superstock

City Park,
Anna Belle Lee Washington

2

SOCIAL STUDIES

Write a description of your favorite food or meal. How does it look, smell, sound, and taste?

3

SCIENCE

Write a description of a rainy day. How does it look, sound, and feel?

 See www.eduplace.com/kids/hme/
for more prompts.

Unit 8: Description **207**

Listening to Poems

In poems, writers use words in special ways to paint word pictures.

 Listen to these poems.

Toaster Time

Tick tick tick tick tick tick tick
Toast up a sandwich quick quick quick
Hamwich
Or jamwich
Lick lick lick!

Tick tick tick tick tick tick––stop!
POP!

Eve Merriam

from *There Is No Rhyme For Silver* by Eve Merriam. Copyright © 1962, 1990 by Eve Merriam. Used by permission of Marian Reiner.

Tommy

I put a seed into the ground
And said, "I'll watch it grow."
I watered it and cared for it
As well as I could know.

One day I walked in my back yard,
And oh, what did I see!
My seed had popped itself right out,
Without consulting me.

Gwendolyn Brooks

from *Bronzeville Boys and Girls* by Gwendolyn Brooks. Copyright © 1956 by Gwendolyn Brooks Blakely. Reprinted by permission of HarperCollins Publishers.

Beetle

A little beetle passed me by,
He didn't make much fuss,
He ran around my garden
Like a tiny yellow bus.

Sylvia Gerdtz

from *Big Dipper Rides Again* edited by Epstein, Factor, McKay & Richards (O.U.P. Australia). Copyright © 1981 by Sylvia Gerdtz. Reprinted by permission of Oxford University Press.

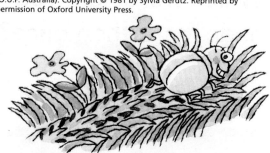

 What words rhyme in each poem? What other kinds of words did you hear?

Listen to these tips.

Tips for Listening to a Poem

★ Listen carefully to the words.
★ Listen for sounds that the words make.
★ Think about what the poem is about.
★ Make pictures in your mind.

Apply It

Now listen to some new poems that your teacher will read. Clap out the beat in each poem.

 What rhyming words and sound words did you hear? Which words did you hear more than once?

Writing a Poem

In a **poem**, you can write about a person, a place, or a thing. You can tell what your topic is like or how you feel about it.

 Listen to these poems.

The Crocus

The golden crocus reaches up
To catch a sunbeam in her cup.

Walter Crane

Smile

It takes a lot of work to frown.
It's easier to smile—
Just take the corners of your mouth
And stretch them for a mile.

Douglas Florian

from *Bing Bang Boing* by Douglas Florian. Copyright © 1994 by Douglas Florian. Reprinted with permission of Harcourt, Inc.

First Snow

Snow makes whiteness where it falls.
The bushes look like popcorn-balls.
The places where I always play
Look like somewhere else today.

Marie Louise Allen

from *A Pocketful of Poems* by Mary Louise Allen. Copyright © 1939 by Harper & Row, Publishers, Inc. Used by permission of HarperCollins Publishers.

Reading As a Writer

✏️▸ Circle the word that tells the color of the crocus.

white   blue   golden

✏️▸ Write words from the poems that rhyme with each of these words.

up _____   smile _____

play _____

✏️▸ What do the bushes look like in "First Snow"?

_____

_____

How to Write a Poem

🖍️▸ Draw what you will write about in your poem.

Unit 8: Description   211

✏️▸ Think about your drawing. Fill in the chart.

Five Senses Chart

My topic is _____ .

See
👁️ _____

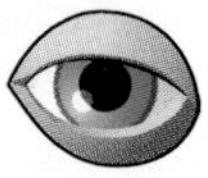

Hear
👂 _____

Smell
👃 _____

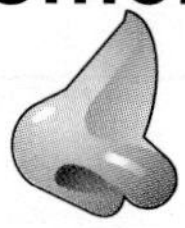

Taste
👄 _____

Touch
✋ _____

✏️▸ Talk about and write sound words and rhyming words for your poem.

_____   _____

_____   _____

_____   _____

Name _____

 Look at Ed's chart and word list. Which words did he use in his poem?

My topic is
feeding the cat.
See
round bowl
Hear
loud meow
Smell
fishy food

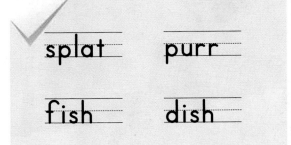
splat   purr
fish   dish

Feeding the Cat

When I feed my furry cat,

I fill his round bowl

With a great big splat.

To me his food

Smells like bad fish,

But he just purrs

And cleans his dish!

 Write your poem. Use words from page 212.

 Talk about your poem with a classmate.

 Make changes to your poem and proofread it. Use the Proofreading Checklist and Proofreading Marks on page 203.

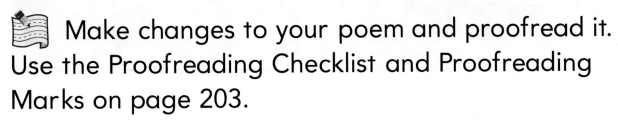 Make a neat copy of your poem and share it.

Giving a Talk

Amy gave a talk to some classmates.

 Look at this picture. Tell what you see.

What do you think Amy talked about? What did she do as she talked?

Name

Listen to these tips.

Be sure your listeners are ready before you begin speaking.

Tips for Giving a Talk

★ Look at your listeners.

★ Use your face and hands.

★ Speak clearly. Be sure everyone can see and hear you.

★ Be sure everyone can see what you are showing.

Apply It

▶ Write a topic that you will talk about.

_____

- -

_____

Draw a picture that you can show as you talk.

Draw yourself using the tips to give a talk.

More Capitalization and Punctuation

Have you read <u>Albert's Ballgame?</u>

Grammar / Mechanics

1 Writing Correct Sentences

One-Minute Warm-Up

How does this sentence begin and end?

The string broke, and the kite got away.

—from The Kite, by Alma Flor Ada

Every sentence begins with a **capital letter**.
A telling sentence ends with a **period**. A question
ends with a **question mark**.

The girl has a kite. **Do you have a kite?**

Try It Out • Think, Speak, Write

Tell how to make each sentence
below correct.

Now write the sentences correctly.

1. she made a kite

She made a kite.

2. it is pretty

3. will it fly

Unit 9: More Capitalization and Punctuation   **217**

1–5. Proofread Mark's riddle. Fix two more mistakes with capital letters and two mistakes with end marks. Then answer the riddle.

Now write the riddle correctly.

Proofreading

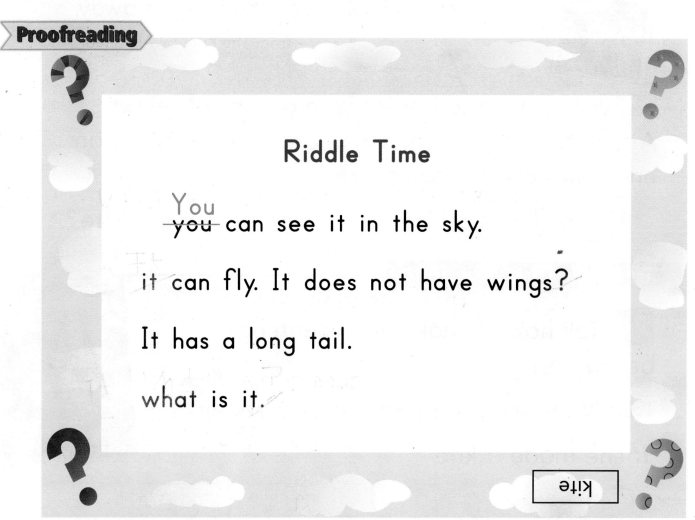

Riddle Time

You
~~you~~ can see it in the sky.

it can fly. It does not have wings?

It has a long tail.

what is it.

kite

Think and Write

Write a sentence about a toy you like.

6. _____

Grammar / Mechanics

2 Exclamations

One-Minute Warm-Up

What do you think the boy might say?
How would he say it?

An **exclamation** is a sentence that shows a strong feeling. It begins with a **capital letter**. It ends with an **exclamation point**.

The clown is very funny!   **His tricks are great!**

Try It Out • Think, Speak, Write

Tell how to make each exclamation below correct.

Now write the sentences correctly.

1. that clown is so tall

That clown is so tall!

2. he is very silly

_____

_____

3. this party is fun

_____

_____

Unit 9: More Capitalization and Punctuation   **219**

1–5. Proofread Rico's sports story.
Fix two more mistakes with capital letters.
Fix two sentences that need exclamation points.

Now write the story correctly.

Proofreading

A Great Soccer Game

Both
~~both~~ teams played hard.

The score was tied.

who would score next? Hooray,

my team got a goal. We won!

it was a great game?

Think and Write

 Write a sentence about a game you have
played. Make the sentence an exclamation.

6. _____

Grammar / Mechanics

3 Titles for People

One-Minute Warm Up

Read the sentence. Which name has a title before it?

The next morning, Arthur ran all the way to Mrs. Wood's house.

—from Arthur's Pet Business, by Marc Brown

A **title** may be used before a person's name. A title begins with a **capital letter** and usually ends with a **period**.

Mr. Smith   **Mrs.** Rose   **Ms.** Lopez
Miss Lee   **Dr.** Jones

Try It Out • Think, Speak, Write

Say each title below. Tell how to make each title correct.

Now write the titles and names correctly.

1. dr Tate

2. mr Green

3. miss Long

1–5. Proofread this list. Fix four more mistakes with titles of people.

Now write the titles and names correctly.

Proofreading

Career Day

Time	Name	Job
9:00	~~mr.~~ Mr. Beck	firefighter
10:00	Ms. Ling	nurse
11:00	dr Dan	vet
1:00	Miss. Small	author
2:00	Mrs Brown	artist

Think and Write

 Write a sentence about your doctor or dentist. Use his or her title.

6. _____

Grammar / Mechanics

4 Book Titles

One-Minute Warm-Up

Read the sentence. What is the title of the library book?

I went to the library and took out a book for me and Enzo called <u>Training Your Pet</u>.

—from <u>Enzo the Wonderfish</u>, by Cathy Wilcox

The first, last, and each important word in a **book title** begins with a **capital letter**. A book title is **underlined**.

I read <u>Sheep in a Jeep</u>.

Try It Out • Think, Speak, Write

 Say each book title below. Tell how to make each title correct.

Now write each book title correctly.

1. tea with milk ___<u>Tea with Milk</u>___

2. the snowy day _____

3. caps for sale _____

1–5. Proofread Matt's book list. Fix four more mistakes with book titles.

Now write the book titles correctly.

Proofreading

My Favorite Books

1. ~~green~~ Green Eggs and Ham

2. The Lion and the mouse

3. The Sleeping Pig

4. The Little House

5. a letter for Amy

Think and Write

Finish this sentence. Write the name of your favorite book.

6. My favorite book is _____

_____

5 Days of the Week

Join the pictures and words to make days of the week.

☀ + day   2 + 💤 + day

There are seven days in a week. The name of each **day** begins with a **capital letter**.

Sunday   **M**onday   **T**uesday   **W**ednesday
Thursday   **F**riday   **S**aturday

Try It Out • Think, Speak, Write

🗣 Say each sentence below. Name the day. Then tell how to make each day correct.

✏️ Draw a line under each day. Then write the days correctly.

1. We paint on monday. 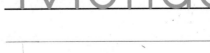 Monday

2. On tuesday we sing. _____

3. I feed Fuzz on friday. _____

1–5. Proofread Amanda's chart. Fix four more mistakes with capital letters.

Now write the days correctly.

Proofreading

My Jobs for the Week

Monday
~~monday~~   I will set the table.

Tuesday   I will make my bed.

wednesday   I will clean the pet cage.

thursday   I will clear the dishes.

Friday   I will make a card for Jess.

saturday   I will rake leaves.

sunday   I will walk with Grandma.

Think and Write

 Write a sentence about your favorite day of the week. Tell why you like it.

6. _____

_____

_____

Grammar / Mechanics

6 Months of the Year

One-Minute Warm-Up

In which months do you go to school? In which months don't you go to school?

There are twelve months in a year. The name of each **month** begins with a **capital letter**.

January	February	March	April
May	June	July	August
September	October	November	December

Try It Out • Think, Speak, Write

Say the name of each month below. Tell how to make each month correct.

Now write the months correctly.

1. june ___June___

2. march _____

3. may _____

4. august _____

1–3. Proofread this class bulletin board.
Fix two more mistakes with capital letters.

Now write the sentences correctly.

Proofreading

We go sledding
~~january.~~ January
in ~~january.~~

In april we like to

walk in the rain.

We see fireworks

in July.

In october we

pick pumpkins.

Think and Write

 Write a sentence about your favorite month.
Tell why it is special.

4. _____

Grammar / Mechanics

7 Holidays

Look at the people in the picture. Name the holiday.

Holidays are special days. The name of each **holiday** begins with a **capital letter**.

My mom gets flowers on Mother's Day.

Try It Out • Think, Speak, Write

Say the name of each holiday below. Tell how to make each holiday correct.

✏️ Now write the holidays correctly.

1. valentine's day —— *Valentine's Day*

2. new year's day _____

3. earth day _____

4. flag day _____

1–5. Proofread Cary's story. Fix three more mistakes with capital letters.

Now write the story correctly.

Proofreading

My Favorite Holidays

Holidays are always fun.

On ~~thanksgiving day,~~ my family

eats a big meal. We hike

with my dad on Father's Day.

My brother and I play little

jokes on april fools' day.

Think and Write

 Write a sentence about a holiday you like.

6. _____

8 Commas in Dates

Big City News

December 18, 2001

Read the date on the newspaper.
What is the month, day, and year?

A **date** tells the month, the number of the day, and the year. A **comma** is used between the number of the day and the year.

My sister was born on May 8, 1998.

Try It Out • Think, Speak, Write

Say each date below. Tell where to put the comma.

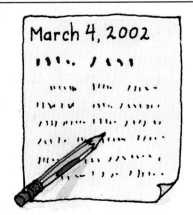

March 4, 2002

Now write the dates correctly.

1. March 4 2002

March 4, 2002

2. December 31 1999

December 31 1999

3. September 11 2001

1–4. Proofread Ana's baby book. Fix three more mistakes with commas in dates.

Now write the dates correctly.

Proofreading

My Special Days

I was born on April 10, 1993.

I took my first step on June 1, 1994.

My first day of school was

August 30, 1995. I rode a bike with

two wheels on July 31, 1999. I lost

my first tooth on October 25, 2000.

Think and Write

 Finish this sentence. Write the month, day, and year that you were born.

5. I was born on _____

_____

9 Commas with Place Names

One-Minute Warm-Up

What is the name of your state?
What city or town do you live in?

Use a **comma** between the name of a **city**
or **town** and the name of a **state**.

My grandmother lives in Tampa, Florida.

Try It Out • Think, Speak, Write

Say each sentence below.
Tell where to put the comma.

Now write the place
names correctly.

1. We live in Troy New York.

Troy, New York

2. We will visit Kent Ohio.

3. Our last stop will be El Paso Texas.

1–3. Proofread Bob's diary. Fix two more mistakes with commas in place names.

Now write the place names correctly.

Proofreading

We left our house in Dover, Delaware yesterday. Today we saw my grandfather in Rockville, Maryland. Tomorrow we will go on rides in Hershey, Pennsylvania. Finally, we will visit an animal park in Jackson, New Jersey. I can't wait!

Think and Write

Finish this sentence. Write the name of the town or city and state where you live.

4. I live in _____

_____.

Words That Sound the Same

Look, Listen, Talk

Some words sound the same, but they are not spelled the same. They also do not mean the same.

Read these sentences about the picture. Which words sound alike?

> The boat is on the sea. The man can see the boat. The green sail is blowing. The woman is having a sale today.

Say the two words below. How are they the same? How are they different? Use each word in a sentence.

road

rode

Apply It

 → Write the word that belongs in each sentence.

1. I have ___one___ sister.

won   one

2. The girl _____ the race.

3. The paint is _____.

blue   blew

4. The wind _____ hard.

5. The _____ is hot.

son   sun

6. Jay is my _____.

7. I _____ the eggs.

beet   beat

8. You can eat a _____.

Name _____

✎▸ Write each sentence correctly.

1. who has lost a hat

_____

_____

2. kate found a hat

_____

_____

✎▸ Write this sentence as an exclamation.

3. she loves ice cream

_____

_____

✎▸ Draw a line under each title. Then write the titles and names correctly.

4. Is mr. Kato your soccer coach?

_____

_____

5. My teacher is mrs Brown. _____

✏️ Write each book title correctly.

_____

6. frog and toad _____

_____

7. a year of birds _____

✏️ Write each special noun correctly.

_____

8. december _____

_____

9. labor day _____

_____

10. tuesday _____

✏️ Write each date and place name correctly.

_____

11. Toledo Ohio _____

_____

12. August 2 2000 _____

✏️ ➤ Write each sentence correctly. Add an end mark. Write capital letters to begin some words.

13. is flag day in june

_____

_____

14. my birthday is on monday

_____

_____

Mixed Review 15–18.

✏️ ➤ Proofread Rosie's story about herself. Fix four mistakes. Two commas are missing. Two words need a capital letter.

> **Proofreading**

I was six years old on March 2 2000. In april we moved to Austin Texas. My new teacher is ms. Jones. My new school is great!

Unit 1: The Sentence

✏️ Circle the naming part in each sentence. Draw a line under each action part.

1. Alex sets the table.

2. Her grandmother brings a vase.

✏️ Write each sentence correctly.

3. tim has a pet pig

_____

_____

4. is the pig brown

_____

_____

Unit 3: Nouns and Pronouns

✏️ Circle the two nouns in each sentence.

5. The horse is in the barn.

6. The boy feeds the hens.

7. This farm sells eggs.

✏️ Write each noun to name more than one.

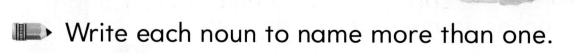

8. toy _____   **9.** hand _____

✏️ Write each special noun correctly.

_____

10. My sister jen took a trip. _____

_____

11. She went to orlando. _____

✏️ Write a pronoun from the Word Box to take the place of each underlined word or words.

_____

12. <u>Dan</u> runs.   _____ runs.

He
She
It

13. <u>Ann</u> walks.   _____ walks.

14. <u>A car</u> honks.   _____ honks.

Unit 5: Verbs

✏️ Draw a line under each verb.

15. Lee plants the seeds.   16. Soon flowers grow.

✏️ Circle the correct verb to finish each sentence.

17. Pedro (plays played) the drums last week.

18. He (plays played) the drums now.

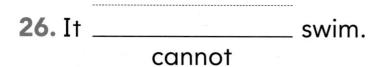

Cumulative Review

✏️ ► Circle the correct verbs.

19. Jack and Dana (sit sits) in a tree fort.

20. The children (is are) up high.

21. Jack (read reads) a book.

22. Dana (eats eat) some food.

23. The sun (was were) in the sky.

24. Now the clouds (hide hides) the sun.

✏️ ► Write a contraction for each word or words.
Then match each sentence to a picture.

25. It _____ short.
            is not

It is the tallest animal.

26. It _____ swim.
            cannot

It can hop.

27. We _____ see it at night.
            do not

We do see it in the day.

✏ Find the words that need capital letters.
Write each sentence correctly.

40. On friday mrs. Smith shops.

_____

_____

41. mother's day is in may.

_____

_____

42. I read <u>dear zoo</u>.

_____

_____

✏ Write a comma in each sentence.

43. Paco lives in Brownsville Texas.

44. His grandmother was born on October 5 1930.

45. I was born on August 6 1995.

46. I started school on September 7 2000.

Writing Instructions

This unit also includes:

Do you know how to paint a flag? I do!

Name

Listening to Instructions

In "Pop-Up Flower Card," the writer tells how to make a special greeting card. What are the steps?

Copyright ©1999 by National Wildlife Federation. Adapted by permission of National Wildlife Federation.

Pop-Up Flower Card

from the writers of <u>Your Big Backyard</u>

Celebrate the coming of spring by making a pop-up flower card! You will need a sheet of heavy paper, crayons or markers, scissors, and glue.

First, fold the sheet of heavy paper in half. Then write a message on the front and decorate it.

Second, cut out the flower pattern on the next page. Then color the flower.

Next, cut out the stem pattern on the next page. Color both sides of it green. Then fold the stem back and forth on the lines. This will help the flower to pop up.

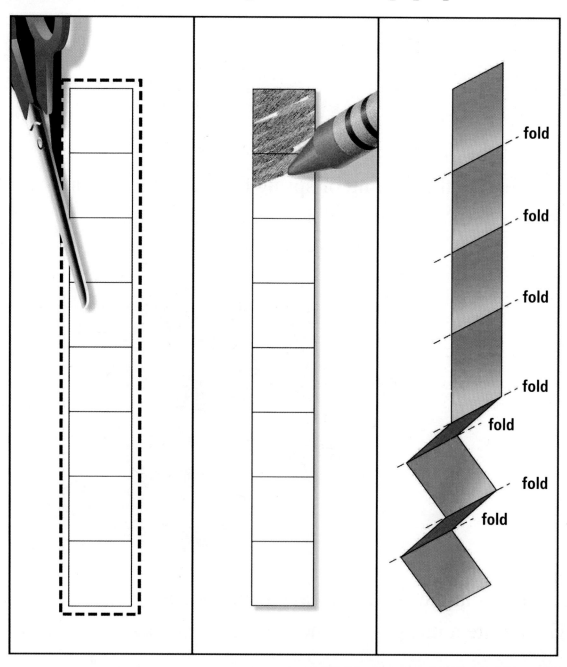

Name

A Published Model

Name

Now, glue the flower to one end of the stem. Glue the other end of the stem to the inside of the card.

Last, close the card so that the stem folds.

Put your card in an envelope and give it to someone special. When he or she opens the card, the flower will pop up!

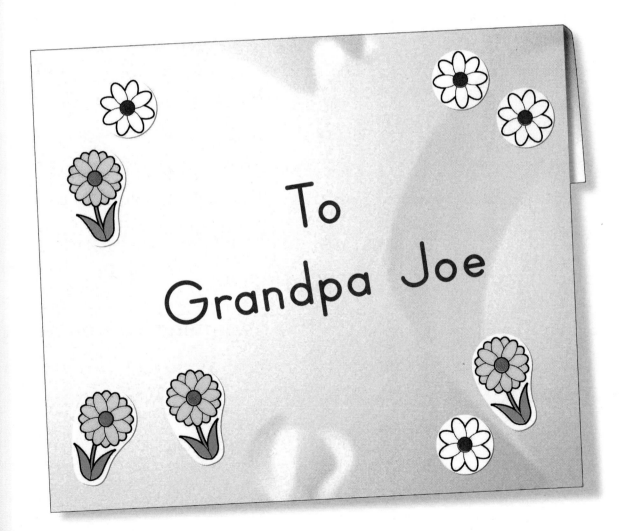

Reading As a Writer

Think About the Instructions

> Read these steps for making the card. Number them in order from 1 to 6.

☐ Cut and color flower.	☐ Glue pieces.
☐ Fold and decorate paper.	☐ Fold stem.
☐ Cut and color stem.	☐ Close card.

> Circle the five words that the writer used to tell the order of the steps.

First   Second   Next   Now   Third   Last

> Which sentence first tells what the instructions are about? Circle the correct answer.

the second sentence   the beginning sentence

Responding

> What did you like about these instructions? Why?

_____

_____

_____

_____

What Makes Great Instructions?

Instructions tell how to do or make something. Remember to do these things when you write instructions.

★ Write an interesting beginning sentence that tells what your paper is about.

★ Write all of the steps in order. Use order words.

★ Write an ending that will make your readers want to follow your instructions.

GRAMMAR CHECK

Add **s** or **es** to most nouns to name more than one.

FINAL COPY

Listen to Hansong's instructions and what W.R. said.

Hansong Qu

You begin with an interesting topic sentence that tells what we will make.

> ## How to Make a Mask
> ### by Hansong Qu
> A mask is easy to make and fun to use. You need a paper plate, scissors, crayons or colored paper, glue, a drinking straw, and tape.

Your steps are in order. You use order words. Good!

> First, fold the plate in half. Next, cut two half circles on the fold for eyes. Then color a face on the plate. You can also cut out decorations and glue them on. Last, tape the straw to the plate for a handle.
> Hold up your mask and have some fun.

Reading As a Writer

 Talk with your classmates.

- What four order words did Hansong use?
- What words in the ending sentence make the reader want to follow these instructions?

 See www.eduplace.com/kids/hme/ for more examples of student writing.

Name _____

Write Instructions

▶ **Choose Your Topic**

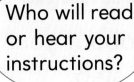 Draw two things that you know how to make or do well.

Who will read or hear your instructions?

[ ] [ ]

Talk about your drawings.

- Which one do you know how to do better?
- Which one would be easier to write about?

Circle the drawing you will write about.

Finish these sentences.

_____

I will tell how to _____.

_____

_____ will read or hear my paper.

Unit 10: Instructions **255**

Explore Your Topic

Think about your instructions. Draw each step.

Draw your steps in the right order.

1	2

3	4

Tell about each drawing. Use order words as you talk. Did you draw every step? Is each step clear?

Make changes to your drawings. Add steps or details.

Name _____

Focus Skill

Order Words

Order words make instructions easy to follow. Look at how Hansong matched order words with the steps in making a mask.

Order Chart		
Number	**Order Word**	**Step**
1	first	fold plate
2	next	cut out eyes
3	then	color or decorate
4	last	tape straw

Try It Together

Talk about how to wash a chalkboard. Use order words. Say the steps in order.

See www.eduplace.com/kids/hme/ for graphic organizers.

Unit 10: Instructions

▶ Plan Your Instructions

✏▸ Look at your drawings. Fill in the chart. Write each step number, order word, and step.

Order Words

first	then
second	now
third	finally
next	last

Order Chart		
Number	**Order Word**	**Step**

Name _____

Beginnings and Endings

Begin with a topic sentence that tells the main idea of your instructions. Tell something interesting about them.

End with a sentence that makes readers want to follow your instructions. Look again at Hansong's beginning and ending.

> A mask is easy to make and fun to use.

> Hold up your mask and have some fun.

Try It Together

Think of sentences to begin and end instructions for making this caterpillar.

Write Your Instructions

First, write an interesting topic sentence. Next, use your Order Chart to write the steps. Last, write an interesting ending.

✓ How Good Are Your Instructions?

 Color the star beside each sentence that tells about your writing.

 I wrote an interesting beginning sentence that tells what my instructions are about.

 I wrote all of the steps in order and used order words.

My ending sentence makes my readers want to follow my instructions.

Be a writing star like W.R.!

 I used what I have learned about capital letters, end marks, spelling, and using words correctly.

Name _____

Revise Your Instructions

 What changes did Hansong make? Why?

First, fold the plate. Then ~~make~~ a face

^in half

color

on the plate. (Next, cut two half circles

on the fold for eyes.)

 Use words from the box, a ∧, and a ᔓ to add and change words. Move a sentence that is out of order.

swing
the ends of the rope

First, two people hold it. Other people

jump over the rope each time it hits the

ground. Next, they move the rope.

 Have a writing conference. See page 262.

Make changes to your writing. Can you color all the stars on page 260 now?

Having a Writing Conference

What are these children saying and doing?

1 Will you help me with my instructions?

Yes, I would like to hear them.

2 Your instructions are clear. Your topic sentence made me want to hear more.

3 Does this step seem like it is in the right order?

Yes, but you could add order words to make the steps easier to follow.

4 Thanks for listening to my instructions and for helping me to make them better.

I am glad I could help.

Name _____

Proofread Your Instructions

What do you look for and do when you proofread? How can you use the Proofreading Checklist and Proofreading Marks to help you?

Proofreading Checklist

- [ ] capital letters
- [ ] end marks
- [ ] spelling

Mark each box on the checklist as you proofread your writing.

Proofreading Marks

- ﹏ take out
- ☰ capital letter

Practice proofreading on page 264 before you proofread your own writing.

Proofread your instructions. Use the Proofreading Checklist and Proofreading Marks.

Remember to add <u>s</u> or <u>es</u> to most nouns to name more than one.

Unit 10: Instructions   **263**

▶ Proofreading Practice

What are the mistakes in this sentence? How did the writer fix them?

                                        buttons
you will need two button?.

> Find mistakes with capital letters, end marks, spelling, and using words.

▶ Find two mistakes in each sentence. Use proofreading marks to fix them.

1. make your mom hapy.

2. help out around the houses.

3. Make your bed evry day

▶ Find eight mistakes. Use proofreading marks to fix them.

clean up your spilled up milk. First, get som paper towel. Next, use the towels. To soak up the milk. Wipe up all the spot! put the towels in the trash.

Name

Publish Your Instructions

Make a neat final copy of your paper. Write a title.

> Be sure you wrote all letters correctly and used good spacing.

Look at Ideas for Sharing on the next page. Share your writing.

Reflect

What did you do best when you wrote your instructions?

_____

_____

_____

_____

What did you learn about writing instructions?

I learned _____ .

Tech Tip Remember to leave space for drawings.

Ideas for Sharing

Write It

⭐ Write each step on a paper strip. Number the steps. Put the strips in order. Make a poster.

Say It

⭐ Read your instructions into a tape recorder. Play the tape for your class.

Show It

⭐ Show your classmates how to do the steps in your instructions.

Name _____

☑ **Writing Prompts**

Use these ideas to write instructions. Think about who will read and follow your instructions.

1 **ART**

Write instructions telling how to draw a dog like this one.

2 **MATH**

Write instructions telling how to make a pattern necklace with pasta. Draw pictures to show the steps.

3 **MUSIC**

Write instructions telling someone how to play a drum or a horn.

See www.eduplace.com/kids/hme/ for more prompts.

Giving Instructions

Maria gave these instructions for playing a game.

Look at the pictures and listen to what she said.

1 To play this game, you will need colored pencils and a sheet of paper.

2 First, draw 4 rows of dots with 5 dots in each row.

3 Next, with a classmate, take turns drawing a line between two dots. Try to make boxes.

4 Last, write your initials in each box you make. The player with the most boxes wins.

Why were Maria's instructions easy to understand? Use them to play the game.

Listen to these tips.

> Make sure you speak slowly and clearly.

Tips for Giving Instructions

★ Tell what your instructions are about.

★ Name the things that are needed.

★ Say the steps in order. Use order words.

★ Show how to follow the instructions.

Apply It

 Think about something you know how to do well. Write the steps you must follow to do it.

Follow the tips above as you say your instructions to a classmate.

Retelling a Spoken Message

Max retells a message he hears.

 Listen to the message. Look at the pictures.

1 "Tell your dad that the field trip has been changed to Friday morning."

2 "What time will we leave?" "We will leave school at 10:00."

3 "I will tell my dad that the field trip has been changed to Friday morning at 10:00."

4 "Dad, Ms. Ramos said the field trip has been changed to Friday morning at 10:00."

 What did Max say and do?

Name

 Listen to these tips.

Tips for Retelling a Spoken Message

★ Listen to the whole message.

★ Listen for important facts and details.

★ Ask questions if something is not clear.

★ Retell the message to the right person.

Apply It

✏ Write a message that you will tell.

_____

- -

_____

- -

_____

- -

_____

Tell your message to a classmate.

Listen as he or she retells it to the group.

Which tips did your classmate follow?

Comparing Media

Newspapers, billboards, television, and radio give information. They are called **media**.

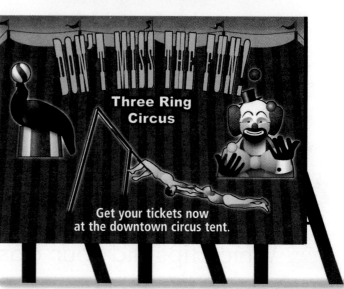 Look at the media below. Listen to the information they give.

Three Ring Circus on Parade

The Three Ring Circus came to town today. People on Main Street were treated to a circus parade. The crowd loved the clowns, jugglers, and animals.

> I'm here on Main Street. The Three Ring Circus has just arrived in town. Behind me, you can see that the circus parade is starting.

> See the show that everybody is talking about. See the juggling clowns, trapeze artists, and amazing animals. Don't miss the Three Ring Circus!

DON'T MISS THE FUN!

Three Ring Circus

Get your tickets now at the downtown circus tent.

Think about the media on page 272.

- Which ones use only words?
- Which ones use pictures and words?
- Which ones use sound?

Apply It

▇▶ Think of some information you can share with your class. Make a poster showing the information.

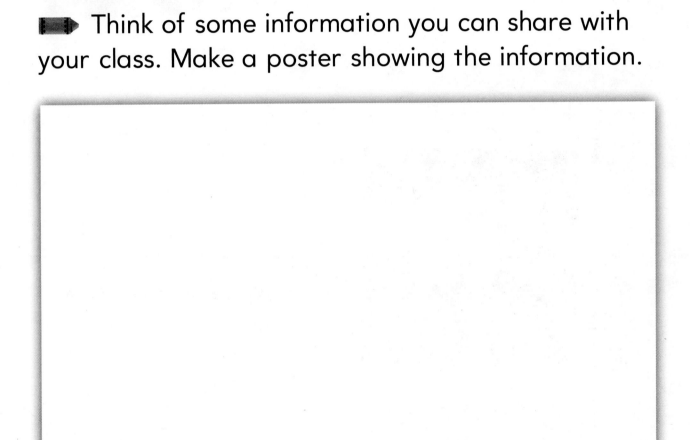

 Write an announcement giving the same information.

 Share your information.

 Talk about your media.

Special Focus

Special Focus on Expressing

Writing an E-mail Message

Page 275

Special Focus on Expressing

Writing to Express an Opinion

Page 278

Special Focus on Informing

Writing a Research Report

Page 284

Name

Writing an E-mail Message

An **e-mail message** is a note that you write and send, using a computer.

 Listen to Ana's e-mail message.

Subject

A Great Movie!

> This is what your message is about.

Type Face ▼

Size ▼

B *I* u

Spelling Check

Dear Grandma,

We saw a movie at school today. It was about a huge bear that was taller than a car. The bear was trying to catch a fish and fell in the river. I know you would like this movie.

> Your message tells a funny detail. I like that!

Send

See you soon!

Ana

Reading As a Writer

✏️▸ Circle the words that name the subject of Ana's e-mail.

    A Good Book!   A Great Movie!

✏️▸ Circle the name of the person who will get Ana's e-mail.

    Grandma   Aunt Jill

> Be sure the person you write to has an e-mail address.

How to Write an E-mail Message

✏️▸ To whom will you write?

_____

_____

✏️▸ List ideas and details that you will write about.

_____

_____

_____

_____

_____

_____

Write your e-mail, using a computer.

1 Type a few words in the subject box. Tell what you will write about.

2 Type a short message. Follow the rules of good writing.

3 Proofread your message. Fix any mistakes.

 Send your e-mail, using a computer.

Remember to check your spelling before you send your e-mail.

Writing to Express an Opinion

When you write an **opinion paper**, you tell why you like or do not like something.

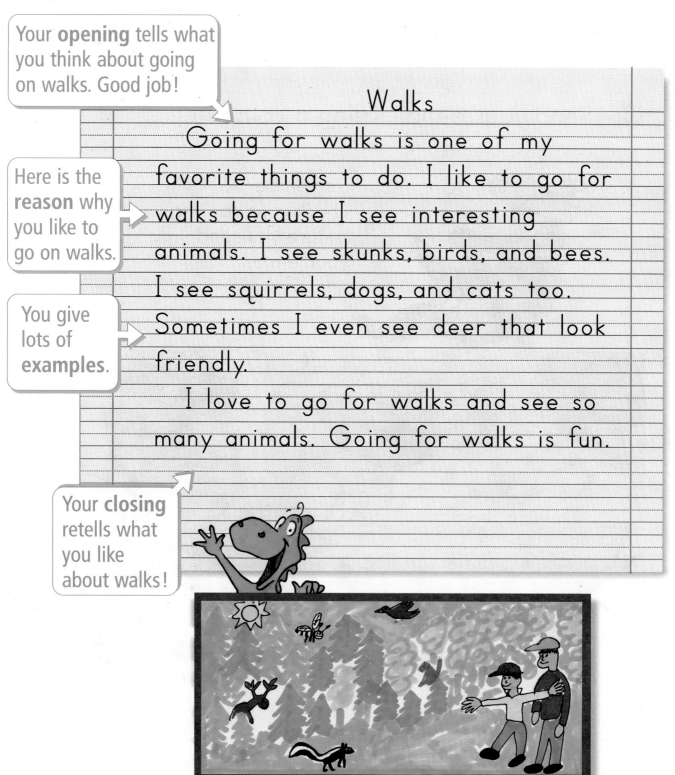 Listen to Dillon's opinion paper and what W.R. said about it.

Your **opening** tells what you think about going on walks. Good job!

Here is the **reason** why you like to go on walks.

You give lots of **examples**.

Your **closing** retells what you like about walks!

Walks

Going for walks is one of my favorite things to do. I like to go for walks because I see interesting animals. I see skunks, birds, and bees. I see squirrels, dogs, and cats too. Sometimes I even see deer that look friendly.

I love to go for walks and see so many animals. Going for walks is fun.

Reading As a Writer

 ▸ Look at Dillon's first sentence. Write the word that lets you know that he likes going for walks.

_____

....

_____

 ▸ Circle the sentence below that tells why Dillon likes to go on walks.

He likes skunks.

He sees many interesting animals.

He walks his dog.

 ▸ Write the names of four animals that Dillon sees on his walks.

_____

....

_____

....

_____

....

_____

How to Write an Opinion Paper

✏️ Think about something that you like a lot. Draw a picture of it. This is your topic.

✏️ Finish this sentence. Write your topic and one thing that you like about it.

I like _____

_____

because _____

_____.

Name _____

Dillon made a plan before he began to write. What did he put in his plan?

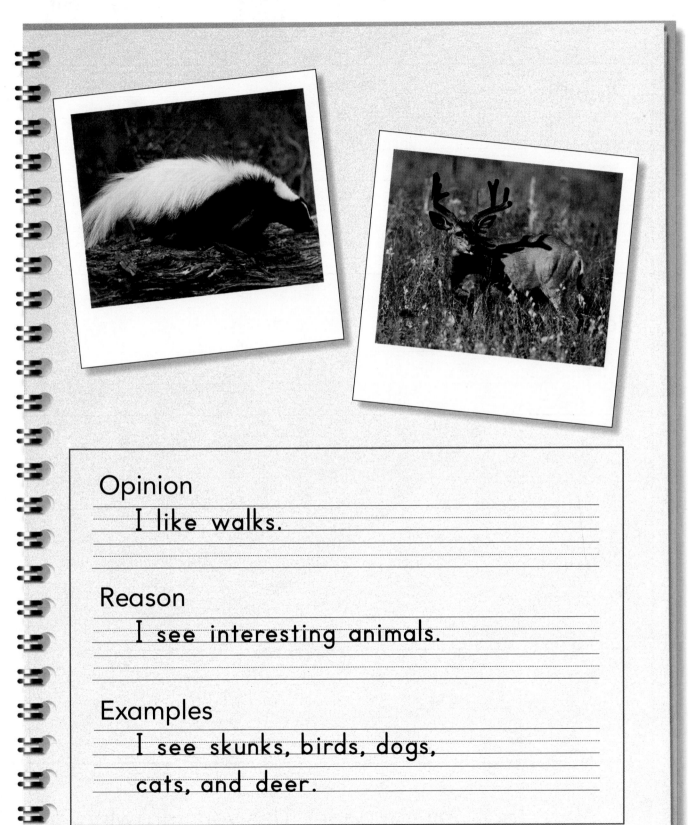

Opinion

   I like walks.

Reason

   I see interesting animals.

Examples

   I see skunks, birds, dogs,
cats, and deer.

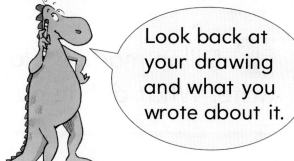

Think about your topic. Fill in this chart to plan your opinion paper.

Look back at your drawing and what you wrote about it.

Opinion

Reason

Examples

Write your opinion paper. Use your drawing and your chart.

Name _____

✔ How Good Is Your Opinion Paper?

✏️ **Color the star beside each sentence that tells about your paper.**

 My opening tells what I think about my topic.

 I wrote a reason for my opinion and some examples.

 My closing retells the reason for my opinion.

 I used what I have learned about capital letters, end marks, spelling, and using words correctly.

 Read your paper to a classmate and talk about it.

Make changes to your paper.

Proofread your paper. Then make a neat final copy and add a title.

Share your paper in an interesting way.

Use the Proofreading Checklist and Proofreading Marks on page 263.

Writing a Research Report

When you write a **research report**, you write facts about a topic.

Listen to Alex's report and what W.R. said about it.

> You tell your topic in the **opening**. Good!

> The **facts** in these sentences answer your **question**.

> Your **closing** is interesting and retells the **main idea**!

A Helpful Insect

The praying mantis is a very helpful insect.

What does a praying mantis look like? It has a thin green and brown body. It can be about the same size as a short pencil. A praying mantis has two wings and six legs. The two front legs have sharp hooks and spines. The praying mantis uses them to catch and hold its food.

People like the praying mantis because it eats bugs. It is a very helpful insect.

Reading As a Writer

✏️ ▸ Circle the picture that shows Alex's topic.

✏️ ▸ Write four facts Alex wrote about his topic.

_____

- -

_____

- -

_____

- -

_____

- -

_____

- -

_____

- -

_____

How to Write a Research Report

 Draw pictures of two animals that you would like to learn about.

 Talk about your pictures with a classmate. Then choose one animal to write about.

 Finish these sentences.

• Is this animal interesting enough?
• Can I find facts about it?

_____

_____

I will write about _____.

_____

_____

I will write my paper for _____ to read.

You will need to find facts about your animal. A **fact** is something that is true or real. An **opinion** is what someone thinks or feels.

 Which sentence tells a fact? Which one tells an opinion?

> A pig has a curly tail.

> I think a pig is cute.

 Look at the chart Alex used to plan his report. What facts did he write to answer his question?

Question and Answer Chart

My topic is ———— a praying mantis ————.

Question —What does a praying mantis look like?—

Answers —green and brown body about the size of short pencil two wings six legs front legs have hooks and spines

---

▌▶ Fill in this chart to plan your report. You can use books to find facts or use a computer to find them.

Question and Answer Chart

My topic is _____.

Question _____

Answers _____

Alex used his chart as he wrote his report. He used his own words to write the facts as sentences. Listen to one fact he found and the sentence he wrote.

Fact

about the size of short pencil

Sentence

It can be about the same size as a short pencil.

Write your research report.

1. Name your topic and tell something about it in your opening.

2. Write your question. Tell what you want to find out about your topic.

3. Write sentences telling facts that answer your question.

4. Write a closing for your report. Tell something interesting about your topic. Retell the main idea.

✓ How Good Is Your Report?

 Read your report. Color the star beside each sentence that tells about your writing.

☆ I wrote an opening and a question about my topic.

☆ I wrote sentences with facts that answer the question.

☆ I wrote an interesting closing. I retold the main idea.

☆ I used what I have learned about capital letters, end marks, spelling, and using words correctly.

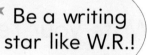 Be a writing star like W.R.!

 Read your report aloud to a classmate. Talk about your writing.

 Think about the changes you could make. Make the changes you want.

290 A Research Report

Proofread your report. Use the Proofreading Checklist and Proofreading Marks to help you.

Proofreading Checklist

- ☐ capital letters
- ☐ end marks
- ☐ spelling

Proofreading Marks

- ℮ take out
- ≡ capital letter

Make a neat final copy of your report. Add a title that tells your topic.

Share your report with the class or someone at home. Show a picture of your animal.

Look for pictures in magazines or draw your own!

Tools and Tips

ABC Order

These letters and words are in ABC order.

a b c d e f g h i j k l m n o p q r s t u v w x y z

dog   hat   nine

Try It Out • Think, Speak, Write

Say the words in each box.

Circle the first letter in each word. Color the frame if the words in a box are in ABC order.

<table>
<tr><td>

1. ⓐpple

   ⓑike

   ⓗat

</td><td>

2. ring

   sun

   tent

</td></tr>
<tr><td>

3. kite

   egg

   doll

</td><td>

4. map

   net

   rug

</td></tr>
</table>

Research and Study Skills

Words in a Dictionary

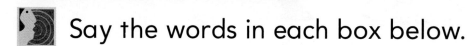

a b c d e f g h i j k l m n o p q r s t u v w x y z

A **dictionary** is a book about words. The words or pictures in a dictionary are in ABC order.

Try It Out • Think, Speak, Write

Say the words in each box below.

Circle the word that comes first in a dictionary.

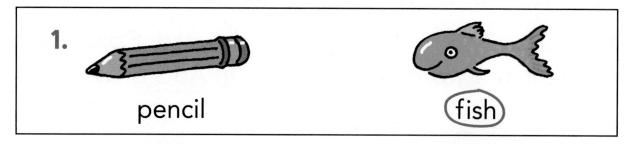

1. pencil   (fish)

2. hat   coat

3. man   saw

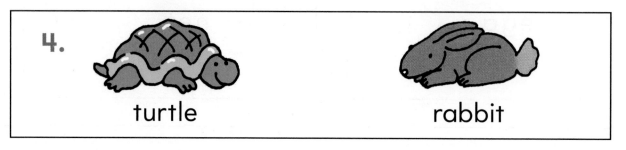

4. turtle   rabbit

Using a Dictionary

Words that begin with the same letter are in the same part of the dictionary.

These words are in the **C** part.

can   **coat**    **cot**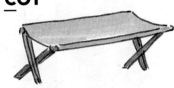

Try It Out • Think, Speak, Write

 Say the words that are in the **B** part of a dictionary.

boat	cat	bat	box
book	girl	bird	bed

Write the letter that names the part of a dictionary where each word is found.

1.

jar _____

2.

key _____

3.

duck _____

4.

boat _____

Research and Study Skills

Using the Library

A **library** is a place where many books are kept. You may borrow these books and take them home.

 Write sentences about what you would see or do in a library.

_____

_____

_____

_____

_____

_____

_____

_____

Parts of a Computer

A **computer** is a machine that you can use to write and draw or to find facts.

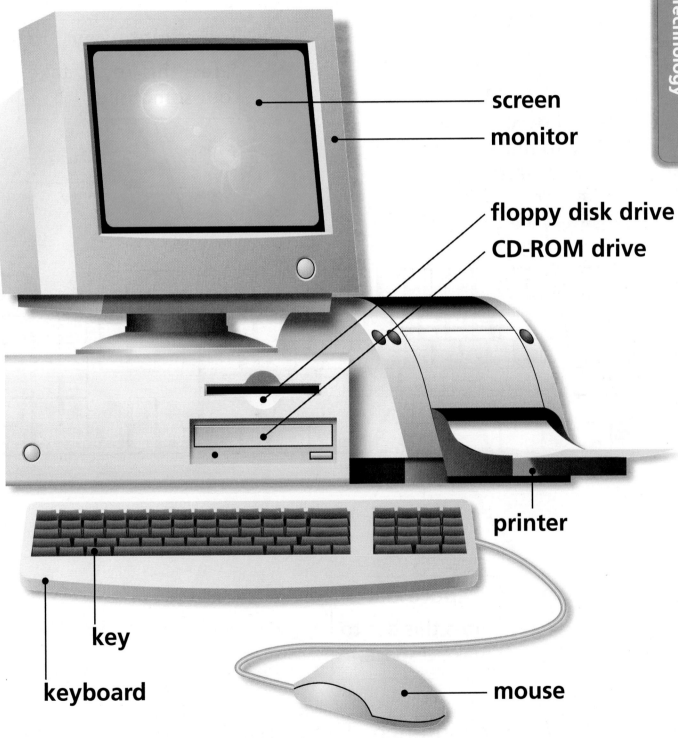

screen

monitor

floppy disk drive

CD-ROM drive

printer

key

keyboard

mouse

Using the Keyboard

The **keyboard** has a key for each letter. Some keys have numbers. Other keys have end marks or other marks.

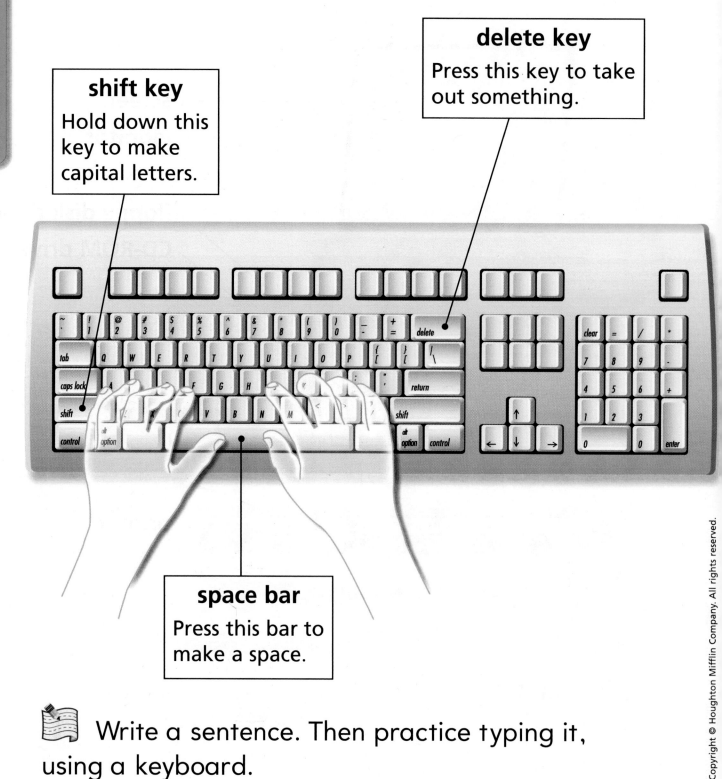

delete key
Press this key to take out something.

shift key
Hold down this key to make capital letters.

space bar
Press this bar to make a space.

Write a sentence. Then practice typing it, using a keyboard.

Using Technology

A Friendly Letter

You write a **friendly letter** to someone you
know. A friendly letter has five parts.

heading — 212 Winter Street
Long Beach, CA 90802
March 25, 2001

Dear Nick, — greeting

My team won the big game! The score
was tied when I came to bat. I hit a home
run! It felt good to do my best.

body

closing — Your friend,
Ana — name

- The **heading** tells your address and the
  day you wrote the letter.

- The **greeting** tells who will get the letter.

- The **body** is the main part.

- The **closing** ends the letter.

- Write your **name** after the closing.

Letter Models

A Thank-you Letter

You write a **thank-you letter** to thank someone for a gift or for doing something nice. A thank-you letter has the same five parts as a friendly letter.

33 Maple Drive
Tampa, FL 33063
October 1, 2001

Dear Aunt Sue,

    Thank you for the book. I can read it by myself. I love the pictures!

Love,
Max

An Invitation

You write an **invitation** to ask someone to come to a party or other event. An invitation tells what the event is. It tells where and when it will be.

Dear _____ Ben _____,

Please come to my

_____ birthday party _____.

Day _____ Sunday, December 18 _____

Time _____ 2:00 _____

Place _____ 10 Cherry Street _____

Your friend,
Jill

Tricky Words to Spell

You use many of these words in your writing. Check this list if you cannot think of the spelling for a word you need. The words are in ABC order.

A
again
always
am
and
are

B
because
before

C
cannot
could

D
down

F
for
friend
from

G
girl
goes

H
have
here
how

I
I'm
it
it's

K
know

L
little

N
name
new
now

O
on
other
our
out

P
pretty

R
really
right

S
said
school
some
something

T
that's
their
there
through
time
tried

V
very

W
want
was
went
were
where
would
write

Y
you
your

Word Bank

People

baby
boy
brother
children
father
friend
girl
man
mother
sister
teacher
woman

Places

airport
beach
city
farm
home
jungle
library
park
playground
pond
school
store
town

Animals

cat
deer
dog
duck
elephant
fox
kangaroo
lion
moose
pig
skunk
tiger
turtle
whale
zebra

Things

apple
ball
bat
bike
car
chalkboard
desk
dish
doll
hat
lunch box
ruler
toy

Actions

catch
chase
cook
cry
draw
drink
eat
fly
hop
jump
kick
laugh
leap
make
paint
play
read
ride
run
sing
skate
skip
sleep
swim
talk
throw
walk
write

Directions

behind
beside
between
down
in
left
on
over
right
under
up

Tastes

fishy
fresh
juicy
salty
smoky
sour
spicy
sweet

Word Finder

Word Bank

Colors
black
blue
brown
green
orange
purple
red
white
yellow

Sizes and Shapes
big
flat
huge
large
little
long
round
short
small
square
tall
thin
tiny
wide

Number Words
zero 0
one 1
two 2
three 3
four 4
five 5
six 6
seven 7
eight 8
nine 9
ten 10

Months
January
February
March
April
May
June
July
August
September
October
November
December

Days
Sunday
Monday
Tuesday
Wednesday
Thursday
Friday
Saturday

Seasons
summer
fall
winter
spring

Holidays
Labor Day
Columbus Day
Thanksgiving Day
Martin Luther
   King, Jr. Day
Valentine's Day
Presidents' Day
Memorial Day
Independence Day

Homophones

Homophones are words that sound alike but have different spellings and meanings.

 beat

 beet

 meet

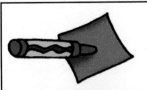 meat

 blue

 blew

 flower

 flour

 tale

tail

 one

 won

 night

 knight

 see

 sea

Word Finder

Using My Picture Dictionary

My Picture Dictionary shows words in ABC order.

 Find each word below in My Picture Dictionary. Write another word that you find under the same letter.

1. bird

boy

2. fan

3. line

4. paint

5. store

Name _____

My Picture Dictionary

Aa

acorn

apple

arm

Bb

bird

boy

bread

Cc

children

circle

coat

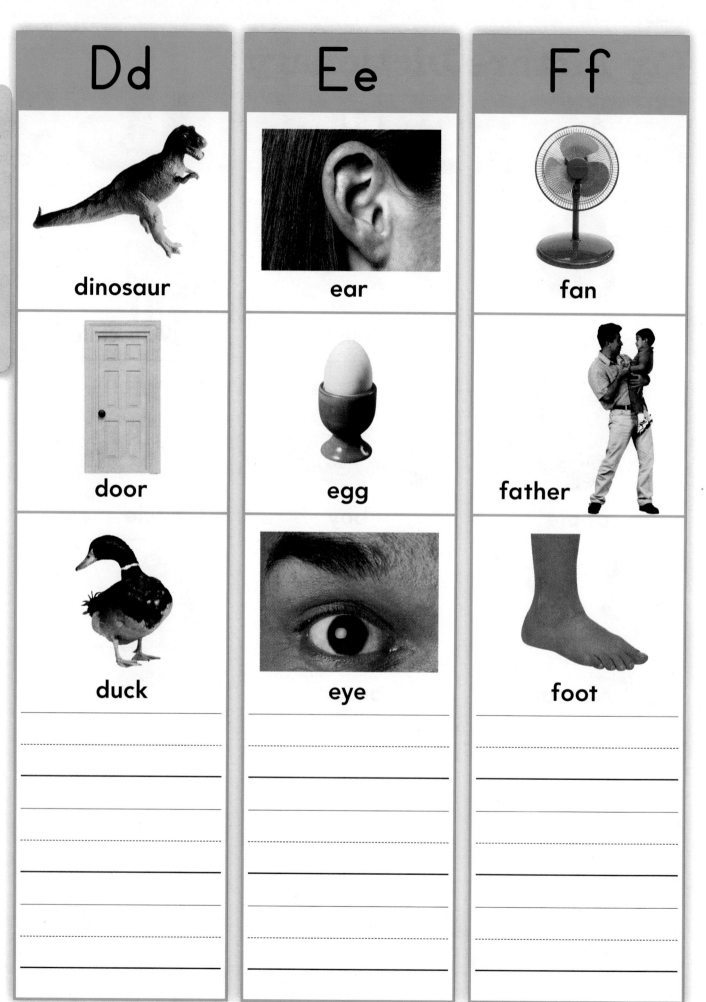

Dd

dinosaur

door

duck

Ee

ear

egg

eye

Ff

fan

father

foot

My Picture Dictionary

Name

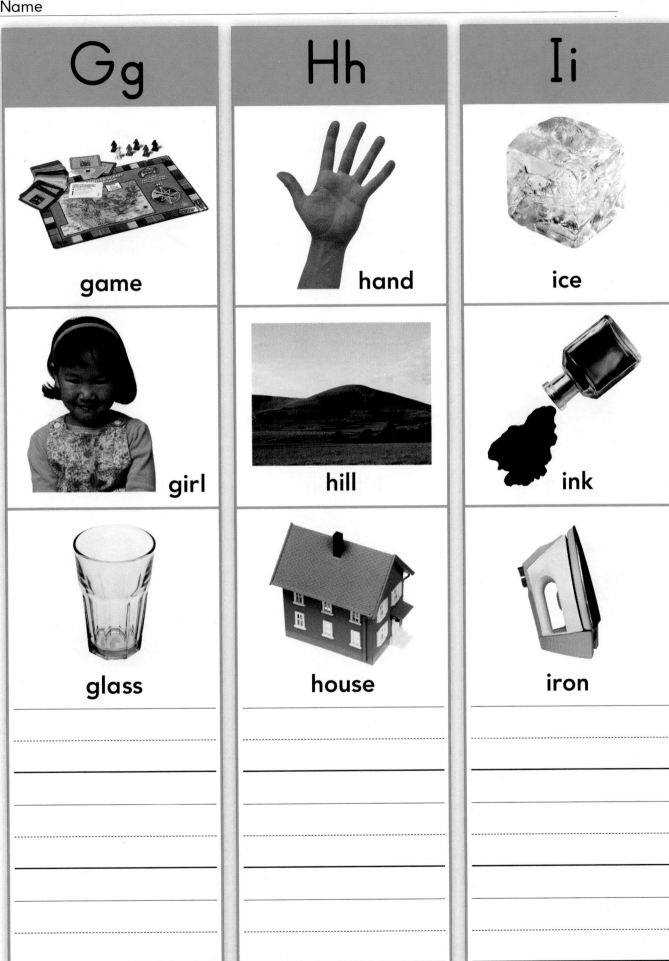

Gg	Hh	Ii
game	hand	ice
girl	hill	ink
glass	house	iron

Jj	Kk	Ll
jar	key	letter
juice	kitchen	line
jump	kite	listen

My Picture Dictionary

310   My Picture Dictionary

Mm

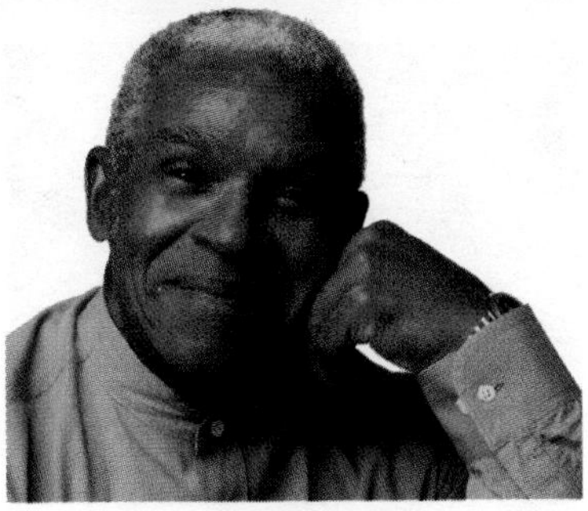

man

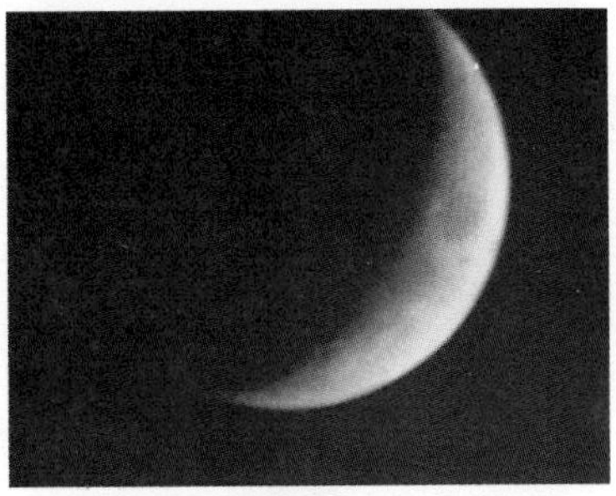

moon

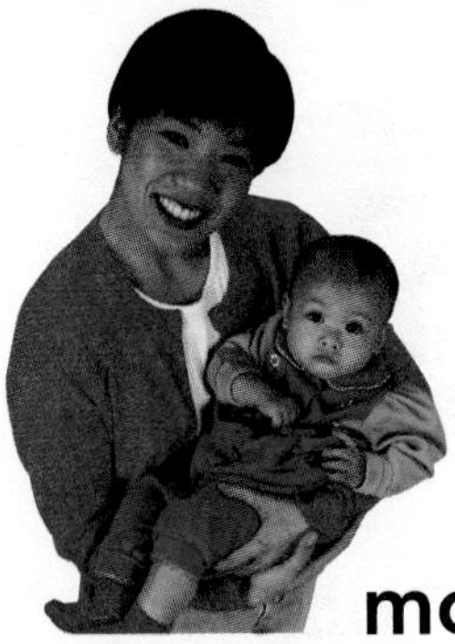

mother

Nn

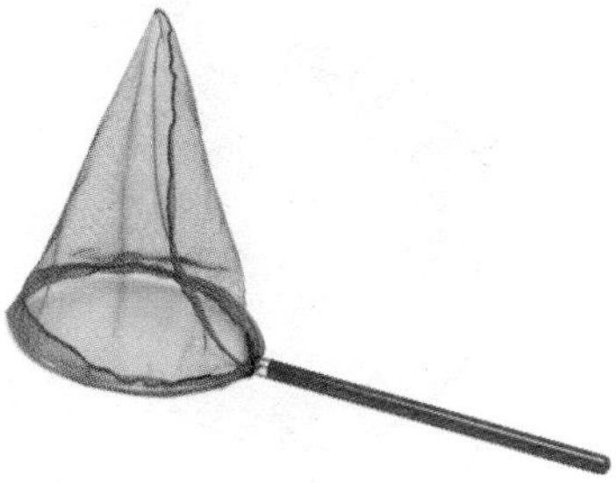

net

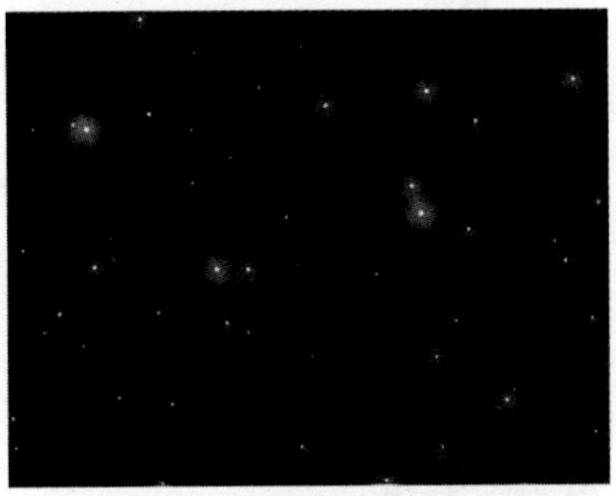

night

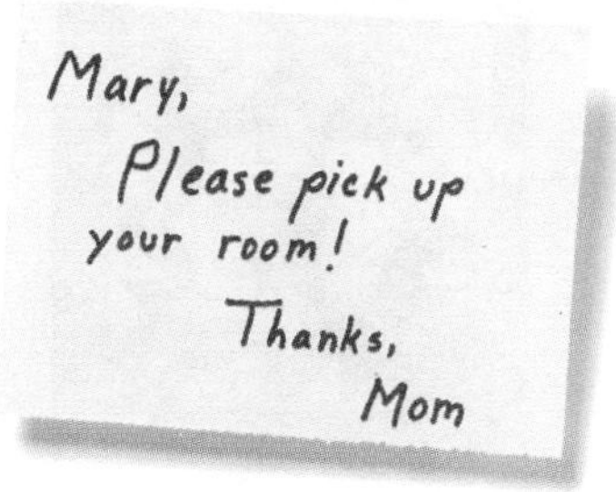

Mary,
Please pick up
your room!
Thanks,
Mom

note

Oo

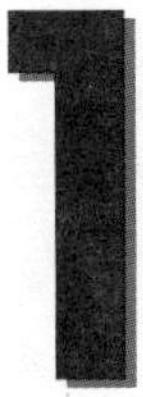

1

one

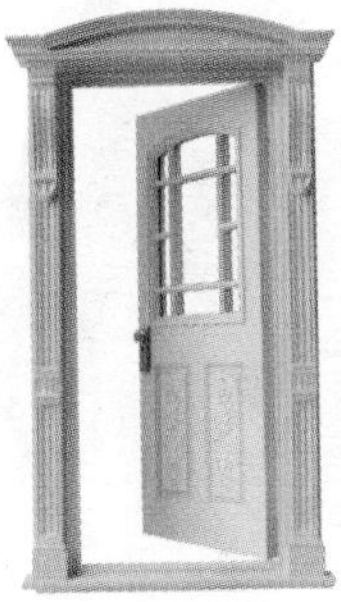

open

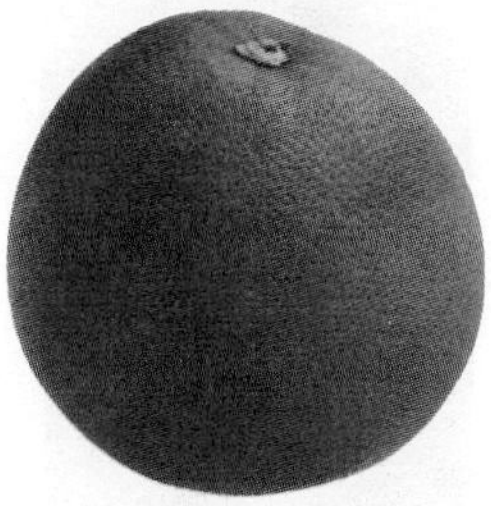

orange

My Picture Dictionary

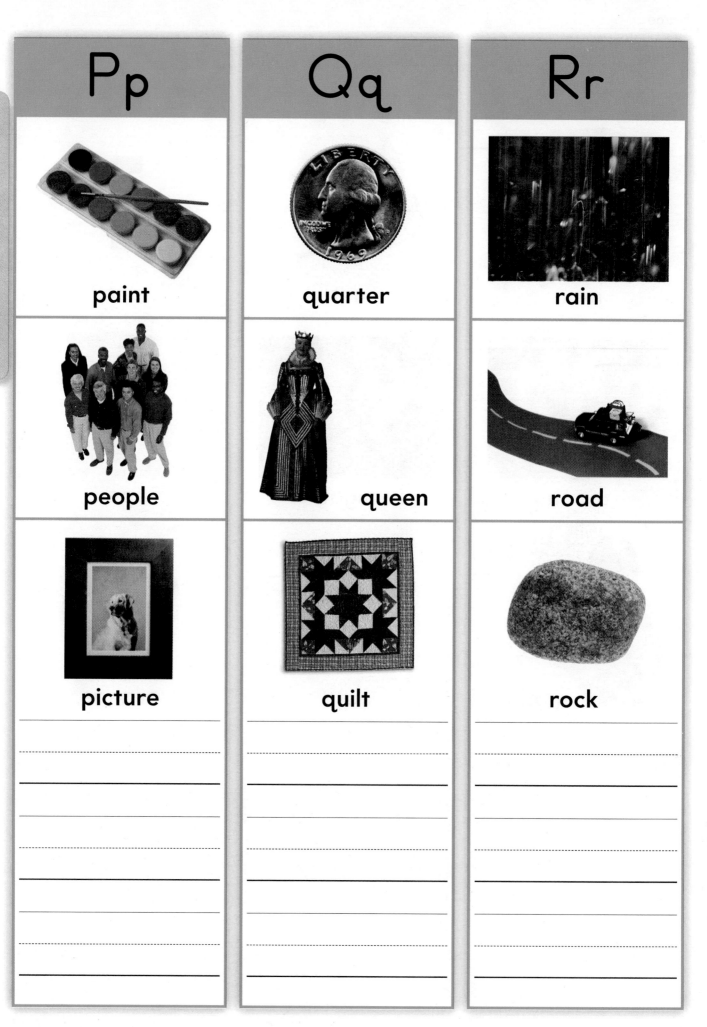

Pp

paint

people

picture

Qq

quarter

queen

quilt

Rr

rain

road

rock

Name _____

Ss

school

sock

store

Tt

table

teacher

two

Uu

umbrella

under

up

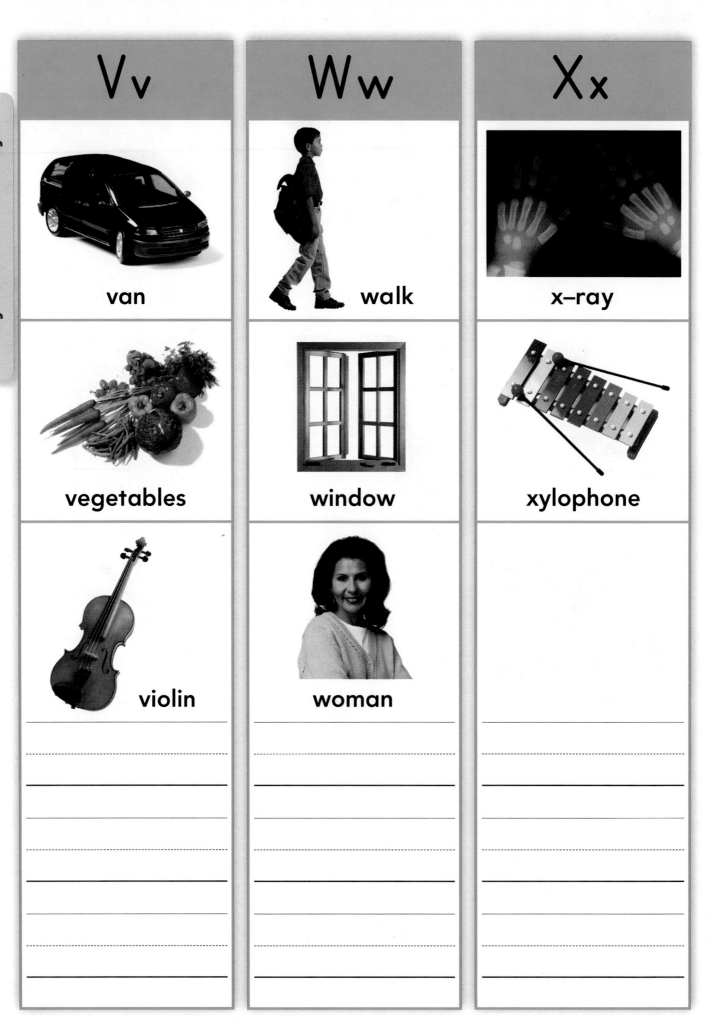

Vv

van

vegetables

violin

Ww

walk

window

woman

Xx

x–ray

xylophone

Name _____

Yy	**Zz**
 yard	 zebra
 year	zipper
yo-yo	 zoo

My Picture Dictionary

Opposites

happy		sad	
tall		short	
thin		thick	
open		closed	
big		little	
noisy		quiet	
hot		cold	
clean		dirty	
light		dark	

Opposites

soft	**hard**
sweet	**sour**
smooth	**bumpy**
slow	**fast**
push	**pull**
laugh	**cry**
throw	**catch**
top	**bottom**
start	**finish**

Handwriting: The Alphabet

A a B b C c D d

E e F f G g H h

I i J j K k L l

M m N n O o P p

Q q R r S s T t

U u V v W w X x

Y y Z z

Handwriting: The Alphabet

Aa Bb Cc Dd Ee
Ff Gg Hh Ii Jj
Kk Ll Mm Nn
Oo Pp Qq Rr Ss
Tt Uu Vv Ww
Xx Yy Zz

A

Abbreviations, 221–222, 237, 245
ABC order, 293–295, 302, 306, 317–318
Addresses, 113
Adjectives
  comparing more than two, 179–180, 185, 189, 194, 204, 243
  comparing two, 179–180, 185, 189, 194, 204, 243
  elaborating with, 99, 104, 151, 159
  identifying, 173–174, 175–176, 177–178, 183–184, 189; Punchouts: *The Adjective Game*
Agreement
  pronoun, 85, 123–124, 135, 188, 241
  subject-verb, 121–122, 123–124, 127–128, 129–130, 135–136, 137, 141, 188, 242
Alphabetical order. *See* ABC order
Antonyms, 181–182, 317–318
Apostrophes
  in contractions, 131–132, 137, 140, 189, 242
Audience, 9–10, 13–14, 15–16, 46, 51–52, 54–55, 95, 98–99, 104, 108–110, 152, 159–161, 163–164, 196, 202, 254, 255, 260, 262, 266, 275–276, 278–279
Author, 166–167, 206

B

be. See Verbs, of being
Beginnings, writing good, 50, 155–156, 159, 259–260, 289, 290
Book report, writing a, 166–169
Brainstorming. *See* Prewriting

C

Capitalization
  of abbreviations, 221–222, 237, 245
  of book titles, 166–167,

223–224, 238, 244, 245
  of days of the week, 225–226, 238, 245
  of first word in a sentence, 30, 34, 40, 53–54, 83, 105, 138, 217–218, 219, 264
  of greetings and closings in letters, 108, 120, 180
  of holidays, 229–230, 238, 245
  of months of the year, 227–228, 238
  of place names, 233–234, 238
  of special nouns, 69–70, 71–72, 80–81, 84, 105, 139, 162, 238, 241
  of titles, 106, 163, 283, 291
  of titles for people, 221–222, 237, 245
Characters
  creating, 150, 151–152, 153–154, 156
Charts
  making, 198, 212, 257–258, 282, 288
  using, 48, 199, 213, 259, 287
Chronological order. *See* Sequence
Class story, 45–56
Closing, in letters, 108, 120, 180, 299
Commas
  after order words, 247, 248, 251, 261
  in letters, 108, 111, 113, 120, 180, 299–300, 301
  separating city and state, 113, 233–234, 245
  separating day and year, 231–232, 239, 245
Communication
  skills, 8–15, 57, 58–59, 114–115, 116–117, 170–171, 208–209, 214–215, 268–269, 270–271
  verbal/nonverbal, 8–16, 58–59, 170–171, 208–209, 214–215, 272–273
  See also Composition; Composition, steps in writing; Listening; Speaking; Viewing

Comparing, 272–273
Composition
  adapting language for, 15–16, 46, 51–52, 54–55, 95, 97–100, 104, 108–110, 152, 154–156, 159–161, 194, 195–197, 253, 260, 275–276, 278–279
  beginnings, good, 50, 155–156, 159, 259–260, 289, 290
  closings, 278, 284, 289–290
  collaborating with others, 19, 45–56, 153, 161, 202, 262
  elaborated sentences, 51–52, 99, 104, 150, 151, 154, 159, 160, 193, 195–196, 200, 261
  endings, 50, 155, 259
  evaluating, 87–96, 106, 143–150, 151–152, 161, 191–193, 195, 200, 202, 205, 209, 252, 253, 254, 260, 262, 265, 283, 290
  exact words, using, 151
  openings, 278, 284, 289–290
  telling about one idea, 45–46, 97–98, 215, 255, 286
  telling enough, 47, 156–158, 198, 256, 280, 283
  See also Composition, steps in writing; Composition, types of; Composition modes
Composition, steps in writing, 43–44
  drafting, 43, 49–50, 103, 159, 199, 259
  prewriting, 43, 45–48, 97–102, 153–157, 196–198, 255–258
  proofreading, 44, 53–54, 105, 162, 203–205, 218, 220, 222, 224, 226, 228, 230, 232, 234, 239, 263–264, 291
  publishing, 44, 54–55, 106, 163–164, 205, 265–266
  revising, 44, 51–52, 104, 160, 201, 261
  See also Drafts, revising; Prewriting; Proofreading
Composition, types of
  book reports, 166–169

Questions

asking and answering, 117, 287

See also Sentences, types of

R _____

Rate of speech, 269

Record knowledge

draw pictures, 255–256

make lists, 17

Reference works. *See* Dictionary

Reflecting, 56, 106, 163, 205, 265

Regular nouns, 67–68

See also Nouns

Repetition, 209

Research and Study Skills, 293–296

Research reports, 284–291

Reviewing written works, 56, 106, 163, 205, 265

Revising strategies

for antonyms, 181–182

definition of revising, 44

for homonyms, 133–134

for homophones, 235–236

for question words, 37–38

for synonyms, 77–78

See also Drafts, revising

Rhyme, 211, 213

Rhythm, 209

Rubrics, 200, 260, 283, 290

S _____

Sensory words, 173–174, 175–176, 177–178, 179–180, 183–184, 189, 191–195, 197–198, 200

Sentences

action parts, 25–26, 39–40, 82, 119–120, 121–122, 138, 186, 240

activities for writing, 30, 34, 168, 184, 186, 217–218, 222, 226, 230, 237, 239, 240, 244, 296, 298

capitalization of first word in, 29–30, 33–34, 40, 53–54, 83, 105, 138, 217–218, 219, 264

identifying, 21–22, 39, 82, 138

naming parts, 23–24, 26, 39–40, 82, 186, 240

punctuating, 30, 34, 36, 40, 41, 138, 217–218, 239, 245

simple, 23–26

types of

complete/incomplete, 28, 39

exclamations, 219–220, 237, 244; Punchouts: *Sidewalk Sentences*

questions, 31–32, 33–34, 35, 37–38, 40, 83, 217–218, 237, 239, 240, 244; Punchouts: *The Sentence Game, Sidewalk Sentences*

telling/statement, 27–28, 29–30, 35, 40, 82, 217–218, 237, 240, 244; Punchouts: *The Sentence Game, Sidewalk Sentences*

Sequence

in instructions, 57, 58–59, 247–251, 252, 254, 256–258, 259–260, 261, 268–269

in a personal narrative, 100–102, 103

in a story, 48, 58–59, 95, 96, 155–158, 159

Sequence of events, 48, 58–59, 100–102

Short story. *See* Personal narrative; Stories

Singular nouns, 67, 121–122, 127–128, 129–130, 187

Speaking

being a good listener and speaker, 8–12, 57, 114–115, 116–117, 208–209, 214–215, 270–271, 272–273

choose/adapt for audience, 11–12

clarify messages, 270–271

to connect experiences/ideas with those of others, 11, 19, 114–115, 164, 206

giving instructions, 268–269

having discussions, 45–47, 116–117

using correct grammar, 21, 23, 25, 27, 29, 31, 33, 35, 61, 63, 65, 67, 69, 71, 73, 75, 119, 121, 123, 125, 127, 129, 131, 173, 175, 177, 179, 217, 219, 221, 223, 225, 227, 229, 231, 233

using correct tense, 125–126, 129–130

using correct volume/rate, 11–12, 114–115, 116–117, 269

See also Communication, skills; Listening, Speaking, Thinking Strategies; Writing conferences

Speech

rate of, 269

volume of, 12, 115, 117

Spelling

homophones, 305

plural nouns, 67–68

proofreading for, 162, 203, 204, 263–264, 291

words often misspelled, 302

Stories

activities for writing, 43–56, 97–107, 153–164, 165

class, 45–56, 59

parts of, 150, 152, 155–158, 165

personal narrative, 87–96, 114–115

sequencing, 48, 58–59, 100–102

using voice, 114–115

See also Personal narrative

Style, 11–12, 95, 108–113, 114–115, 116–117, 166–169, 210–213, 269, 275–277, 278–283

Subject of a sentence. *See* Sentences, naming parts

Subject-verb agreement. *See* Agreement, subject-verb

Summarize, 270–271

Supporting details, 99, 104, 150, 151, 154, 159

Synonyms, 77–78

T _____

Technology, using, 106, 163, 164, 205, 275–277, 287, 297–298

Acknowledgments *continued*

Book Report

Shoes Like Miss Alice's by Angela Johnson, illustrated by Ken Page. Jacket illustration copyright ©1995 by Ken Page. Reprinted by permission of Orchard Books, New York. All rights reserved.

One Minute Warm-up

Arthur's Pet Business by Marc Brown, published by Little, Brown and Company, 1990. Used by permission.

Enzo the Wonderfish by Cathy Wilcox, published by Ticknor & Fields, 1993. Used by permission of Houghton Mifflin Company.

Frog and Toad All Year by Arnold Lobel, published by HarperCollins Publishers, 1976. Used by permission.

I Went Walking by Sue Williams, illustrated by Julie Vivas, published by Gulliver Books, 1989. Used by permission.

The Kite by Alma Flor Ada, illustrated by Vivi Escriva, published by Santillana Publishing Company, Inc., 1992. Used by permission.

Student Writing Model Contributors

Juan Arias, Dillon Bowen, Alexander Davis, Jhogel Florentino, Nicole Jackson, Hansong Qu, Kristin Roe, Katrice Willis, and the students in Liz Menendez's class at the Claremont Community School, Bronx, New York.

Credits

Illustrations

Christiane Beauregard: 83 (t), 94, 130, 132 (t), 133 (t), 134, 139 (t), 183 (t), 188 (b), 218, 227–228, 232 (insets), 233 (b), 239 (t), 242 (b), 243 (b), 301 **Lizi Boyd:** 166 (r) **Liz Callen:** 80, 81, 82 (t), 108 (b), 117 (b), 132 (b), 139 (b), 152 (b), 153–154, 181, 183 (b), 185, 186 (b), 187 (b), 189 (b), 220, 224, 225 (t), 226, 238, 239 (b), 244 **Chris Demarest:** 138 (t), 173–176, 177 (t), 187 (t), 188 (m), 235–236, 295 **Tuko Fujisaki:** 39 (m), 79 (b), 170, 208 **Myron Grossman:** 240 (t), 243 (t), 245 **Jennifer Beck Harris:** 83 (b), 107, 141 (b), 165, 186 (m), 207, 267 (t), 293–294, 296, 305 **John Hovell:** 7, 120, 122, 124 (bkgrd.), 126, 128, 137 (bkgrd.), 180 (bkgrd.), 197–198, 199 (l&r), 201 (b), 212, 213 (tl), 222, 232 (bkgrd.), 233 (t), 234 (bkgrd.), 247–251, 272, 275, 281, 297, 298 **Anne Kennedy:** 43–44, 46, 48, 50, 52–53, 55–56, 57 (t), 59 (t), 95–97, 100–103, 104 (r), 105 (b), 106, 108 (t), 113, 115, 117 (t), 150–152 (t), 156–160, 161 (t), 162–164, 166 (l), 168–169, 194–195, 199 (b), 200, 201 (t), 202 (t), 203–206, 209, 215, 253–256, 258, 260, 262 (t), 263–266, 269, 271, 275 (r), 276–277, 278 (tl), 282–284, 286, 291, 316 **Stephen Lewis:** 21–28, 38, 39 (t & b), 40, 41 (t), 99, 104 (l), 105 (t), 121, 124 (inset), 125, 136, 140 (t), 155, 161 (b) **Ginna Magee:** 71–76, 79 (t), 82 (b), 84–85, 210, 213, 270 **Diane Paterson:** 14, 19, 61–70, 77, 149, 167, 177 (b), 179, 180 (inset), 182, 184, 186 (t), 188 (t), 189 (t), 219, 221, 225 (b), 229–231, 234 (inset), 237, 240 (b), 241, 242 (t) **Mick Reid:** 317, 318 **George Ulrich:** 29–37, 41 (b), 59 (b), 78, 119, 123, 127, 129, 131, 135, 137 (inset), 138 (b), 140 (b), 141 (t&m), 202 (b), 257, 262 (b)

Photographs

Cover Photograph: Keren Su/Index Stock Imagery.

Fine Art: 165 Christie's Images/Superstock **207** Anna Belle Lee Washington/Superstock.

Getting Started: 3 Index Stock Imagery **4** VCG **5** (t) Art Wolfe/Tony Stone Images **5** (b) Mug Shots/The Stock Market **6** (t) Anthony Edgeworth/The Stock Market **6** (b) Jim Cummings/FPG **7** (l) Mary Kate Denny/Tony Stone Images **7** (m) Tim Davis/The Stock Market **7** (r) Tom and DeeAnn McCarthy/The Stock Market **8** (tl) Jilly Wendell/Tony Stone Images **8** (tr) Ed Bock/The Stock Market **8** (bl) Kalunzy/Thatch/Tony Stone Images **8** (br) Mark Tuschman/The Stock Market **9** (all) Parker/Boon **11** (tl & tr) Joel Benjamin **11** (bl & br) Parker/Boon **13** (tl) Frank Siteman/Stock Boston **13** (tr) Lawrence Migdale/Stock Boston/PictureQuest **13** (bl) David Young-Wolff/PhotoEdit/PictureQuest **13** (br) Joseph Nettis/Stock Boston/PictureQuest **15** (all) Joel Benjamin **17** HMCo. Digital Studio **18** HMCo. Digital Studio. **Unit 1: 20** Keren Su/Index Stock Imagery. **Unit 2: 42** Index Stock Imagery **45** Joel Benjamin **49** Joel Benjamin **51** Joel Benjamin **54** Joel Benjamin **57** (b) HMCo. Digital Studio **58** (all) Abbe Boon. **Unit 3: 60** Jeff Greenberg/PhotoEdit/PictureQuest **80** Peter Correz/Tony Stone Images. **Unit 4: 86** Lori Adamski Peek/Tony Stone Images **98** Joel Benjamin **103** Joel Benjamin **106** Joel Benjamin **107** Philip James Corwin/Corbis **109** (tr) Joel

Photographs *continued*

Benjamin **109** (bl) Nik Wheeler/Corbis **109** (br)Yoav Levy/Phototake/PictureQuest **114** (all) Joel Benjamin **116** Joel Benjamin. **Unit 5: 118** Telegraph Colour Library/FPG **126** Lawrence Migdale/Stock Boston/PictureQuest **135** Photodisc. **Unit 6: 142** VCG **159** Joel Benjamin **164** (t) HMCo. Archive **164** (m&b) Joel Benjamin. **Unit 7: 172** Art Wolfe/Tony Stone Images **178** (all) Photodisc **184** Sara Gray/Tony Stone Images **185** James L. Amos/Corbis. **Unit 8: 190** Mug Shots/The Stock Market **196** (l) Arthur Beck/The Stock Market **196** (r) Kevin R. Morris/Corbis **197** (t) Photodisc **197** (b) Renee Lynn/The Stock Market **205** Joel Benjamin **206** (t) Abbe Boon **206** (m) Joel Benjamin **206** (b) Abbe Boon **209** Joel Benjamin **214** Joel Benjamin. **Unit 9: 216** Anthony Edgeworth/The Stock Market **217** Roger Ress Meyer/Corbis **223** Jack Monnier/Tony Stone Images. **Unit 10: 246** Jim Cummings/FPG **259** HMCo. Digital Studio **261** HMCo. Archive **265** Joel Benjamin **266** (all) Joel Benjamin **267** (b) HMCo. Digital Studio **268** Joel Benjamin. **Special Focus Unit: 274** (t) Mary Kate Denny/Tony Stone Images **274** (m) Tim Davis/The Stock Market **274** (b) Tom and DeeAnn McCarthy/The Stock Market **277** Comstock **279** Ron Thomas/FPG **281** (l) D. Robert Franz/Corbis **281** (r) Photodisc **284** Gail Shumway/FPG **285** (all) Photodisc **287** Joel Benjamin **289** Joel Benjamin **291** Joel Benjamin **Tools & Tips: 306** (t to b) Photodisc, HMCo. Archive, Joel Benjamin, Artville, HMCo. Archive **307** (row 1, l to r) Photodisc, Photodisc, Rubberball Productions, (row 2, l to r) Artville, Rubberball Productions, Joel Benjamin, (row 3, l to r) Rubberball Productions, Photodisc, Joel Benjamin **308** (row 1, l to r) HMCo. Archive, Photodisc, HMCo. Archive, (row 2, l to r) HMCo. Archive, Corbis Royalty Free, Corbis Royalty Free, (row 3, l to r) Photodisc, Photodisc, Tony Scarpetta **309** (row 1, l to r) HMCo. Archive, Photodisc, HMCo. Archive, (row 2, l to r) Photodisc, Photodisc, Photodisc, (row 3, l to r) HMCo. Archive, HMCo. Archive, Photodisc **310** (row 1, l to r) HMCo. Archive, Photodisc, HMCo. Archive, (row 2, l to r) Photodisc, HMCo. Archive, Joel Benjamin, (row 3, l to r) Tracey Wheeler, HMCo. Archive, Photodisc **311** (row 1, l & m) Photodisc, HMCo. Archive, (row 2, l to r) Image Ideas, Photodisc, Stock Market, (row 3, l to r) Corbis Royalty Free, HMCo. Archive, Artville **312** (row 1, l to r) Artville, HMCo. Archive, Photodisc, (row 2, l to r) Photodisc, Corbis Royalty Free, HMCo. Archive, (row 3, l to r) Photodisc, Michelle Joyce, HMCo. Archive **313** (row 1, l to r) HMCo. Archive, HMCo. Archive, Stockbyte, (row 2, l to r) HMCo. Archive, (ml) Comstock KLIPS, (mr) Image Ideas, Joel Benjamin, (row 3, l & r) HMCo. Archive, Eyewire **314** (row 1, l to r) HMCo. Archive, Rubberball Productions, Photodisc, (row 2, l to r) HMCo. Archive, Photodisc, HMCo. Archive, (row 3, l & m) Photodisc, Photodisc **315** (row 1, l & m) HMCo. Archive, Raymond Gehman/Corbis, (row 2, l & m) Ken Karp, Michelle Joyce, (row 3, l & m) Photodisc, Joel Benjamin, (far right) Ken Karp.